Movie Stars and Sensuous Scars

Movie Stars and Sensuous Scars

◆

Essays on the Journey from Disability Shame to Disability Pride

Steven E. Brown

People with Disabilities Press Series
Stanley D. Klein, Ph.D., Series Editor

iUniverse, Inc.
New York Lincoln Shanghai

Movie Stars and Sensuous Scars
Essays on the Journey from Disability Shame to Disability Pride

iUniverse books may be ordered through booksellers or by contacting:

iUniverse
2021 Pine Lake Road, Suite 100
Lincoln, NE 68512
www.iuniverse.com
1-800-Authors (1-800-288-4677)

ISBN-13: 978-0-595-28893-9 (pbk)
ISBN-13: 978-0-595-82267-6 (ebk)
ISBN-10: 0-595-28893-6 (pbk)
ISBN-10: 0-595-82267-3 (ebk)

Printed in the United States of America

Contents

Part IV   Profiles

Part V   Disability Rights and Culture

Part VI   *Endings and Beginnings*

ACKNOWLEDGEMENTS

We gratefully acknowledge permission to include in this book previously published articles. All have been revised for inclusion in this book. They first appeared in the following publications:

"American Apartheid," (Progressive Independence, Norman, OK) *Advocate*, (January 1988), 1.
http://www.progind.org/

"Creating a Disability Mythology," *International Journal of Rehabilitation Research*, 15, (Winter 1992), 227-33.

"The Curb Ramps of Kalamazoo: Discovering Our Unrecorded History," *Disability Studies Quarterly*, 19 (3), (Summer 1999), 203-05.
http://www.cds.hawaii.edu/dsq/

"Death and Life," co-authored with Lillian Gonzales Brown, *MAINSTREAM: Magazine of the Able-Disabled*, 20 (1), (Sept. 1995), 29-31. (No longer publishing)

"Deviants, Invalids, and Anthropologists," *Disability and Rehabilitation: An International, Multidisciplinary Journal*, 18 (5) (May 1996), 273-75.
http://www.tandf.co.uk

"Dis-Ing Definitions," *MAINSTREAM: Magazine of the Able-Disabled*, 21 (10), (Aug. 1997), 22, 26-27, 29.

"Gentle, Angry People," as "A Gentle, Angry People: They Won't Abandon Coalition-Building," *DISABLED USA* ([19]86/1-2), 39-41. (No longer publishing)

"A Healing Journey," *Disability Life*, 2 (2), (May/June 2000), 21-30. (No longer publishing)

"Hidden Treasure," *Gaucher's Disease Registry Newsletter*, (Oct.–Nov. 1984), 4, 5, 6. http://www.gaucherdisease.org/

"Hooked on Symptoms: Drug Abuse from a Disability Perspective," *Independent Living*, (Aug./Sept. 1990), 63-66. (No longer publishing)

"I Was Born (In a Hospital Bed)—When I Was Thirty-One Years Old," *Disability and Society*, 10, (1), (1995), 103-110. Funding from the World Institute on Disability and the National Institute on Disability Rehabilitation and Research grant #H133B00006-90 made this article possible. http://www.tandf.co.uk

"In Freedom, Frank," *MAINSTREAM: Magazine of the Able-Disabled*, 22 (9) (June/July 1998), 32, 34.

"Oh, Don't You Envy Us Our Privileged Lives?" A Review of the Disability Culture Movement," *Disability and Rehabilitation: An International, Multidisciplinary Journal*, 19 (8) (August 1997), 339-49. http://www.tandf.co.uk

"Movie Stars and Sensuous Scars," *MAINSTREAM: Magazine of the Able-Disabled*, 21 (5), (Feb. 1997), 26, 28, 31.

"Rethinking the Disability Agenda," as "Who Benefits?" *New Mobility: Disability Culture & Lifestyle*, 8 (51), (December 1997), 12. http://www.newmobility.com/

"Some Reflections on the ADA," *Ragged Edge: The Disability Experience in America*, 19 (5) (Sept.—Oct. 1998), 15-16, 45. http://www.ragged-edge-mag.com/

"The Truth about Telethons," *OCCD Newsletter*, VII, (Summer/Fall 1985) 4-5. (No longer publishing)

"The Walkout," *Disability Rag*, 6, (9), (September 1985) 39-40. http://www.ragged-edge-mag.com/

"We Are Who We Are...So Who Are We?" *MAINSTREAM: Magazine of The Able-Disabled*, 20 (10), (Aug. 1996), 28-30, 32.

"Zona and Ed Roberts: Twentieth Century Pioneers," *Disability Studies Quarterly* 20 (1) (Winter 2000), 26-42. http://www.cds.hawaii.edu/dsq/

Lyrics are used by permission of the following:

Blacking Up
by Mat Fraser
http://www.matfraser.com/

Singing for our Lives
by Holly Near, c 1979 Hereford Music (ASCAP).
http://www.hollynear.com

Speaking Hands, Hearing Eyes
Words and music by Judy Small, ©1984 Crafty Maid Music.
http://www.judysmall.net

PREFACE

Welcome to my life. I've been writing about it for more than thirty years now. I penned the oldest essay in this collection, "Hidden Treasure," when I was seventeen. The most recent, "A Healing Journey," I composed in my late forties.

I have spent the past thirty years of my life becoming. In my early twenties, I became a historian, earning a doctoral degree. In my early thirties, I became an activist, working in the disability rights movement. In my early forties, I became a promoter, convinced that the world needed to understand the idea of disability culture. In my early fifties, I became interested in healing. I'm still learning what that entails.

The essays in this book reflect the intellectual and activist wanderings of a scholar who thinks about how his own life has an impact on the greater population and visa versa.

I've divided this book into six sections. They are: *Personal Stories; The Disability Rights Movement; Disability Culture; Profiles; Disability Rights and Culture;* and *Endings and Beginnings.*

I begin with *Personal Stories* because it's difficult to understand how I came to my later views and opinions without knowing how my own history shaped me. I follow that with the *Disability Rights Movement* because as I grew into young adulthood, I became an active participant and thinker about that cause. This work led me to a belief in *Disability Culture,* the section that follows. Along the way, I've met many fascinating people and had a chance to write about a few of them. I've included these essays in the *Profiles* section. In the decade of the 1990s I did a lot of traveling, both in the United States and internationally. I discuss those experiences in *Disability Rights and Culture.* Finally, I conclude with another personal essay. This one combines disability rights, personal stories, and my newfound interest in healing. I've therefore labeled it *Endings and Beginnings.*

So this is a collection of personal reminiscences, contemplations, historical documentation, poems, and reflections of a life lived, like most of ours are, that is both scarred and sensual. I hope these pieces speak in some way to your life and your own healing journeys.

As with life itself, there are repetitions from one story to another. Some repetition has been retained in the belief that any of these essays may be used independently from the rest if desired.

Many people have contributed to the development of this book. I am most grateful to those whose names appear in the text and who have given me permission to become a part of their lives, and who in turn have become a part of mine. I thank all the people who have supported, and published, my writings over the years. I thank a legion of people who have read and commented on these writings. While I have not always followed suggestions, I have always listened and appreciated.

Lisa Galloway did an admirable job of proofreading and editing the manuscript.

I dedicate this work to the millions of people with disabilities around the world who still linger in squalid lives of desperation because of societal prejudices. I thank my daughter, Aimee, for her love and her enthusiasm for my writing. Finally, I thank my wife, Lillian Gonzales Brown, who contributes so many things, including the concepts and wording for the subtitle of this book, and who stimulates my thinking about all our journeys.

I love you.

Steven E. Brown
Honolulu, HI
June 2003

PART I
Personal Stories

INTRODUCTION: GAUCHER DISEASE: A PERSONAL HISTORY

[I wrote this piece in 1989. Lots of people ask me about my disability and how it has affected my life. I tried to address them in this never before published essay. I begin the book with this essay because it explains many causes and effects of my disability and how these have impacted my thinking about my life and work.]

I was born, the first of three children, in Manitowoc, Wisconsin on October 26, 1951. I have no clear memories from my earliest years, though I do have vague mind pictures of walks with my father along a waterfront.

My parents, my younger brother and I moved to Kalamazoo, Michigan when I was four. Two years later, when I was about six, I began to limp on my right leg for no apparent reason. Physicians in Kalamazoo could not diagnose the source of the pain causing the limp. I boarded my first plane, with my mother, pregnant with my sister, and my paternal grandmother, to travel to the Mayo Clinic in Rochester, Minnesota, where my father's family had a history of medical visits.

A biopsy revealed I had Gaucher (pronounced Go-shay) Disease (GD). At that time, in the late 1950s, little had been discovered about this disease, first described by a French medical student, Philippe Gaucher, in 1882.

The Mayo Clinic doctor informed my mother that people inherited GD. A combination of recessive genes needed to be passed on by both parents. If a child received a recessive gene and a dominant gene, that child would carry the recessive GD gene, but not have the disease. If they received two dominant genes, the child would neither have GD nor be a carrier. If a child, like myself, received recessive genes from both sets of parents, they would both have and be a carrier of GD. Both my parents fit into that category of carrying a recessive gene. Neither had heard of GD.

The doctors could not go much beyond this genetic explanation because they did not know much more than that. The doctor at the Mayo Clinic informed my mother that bone pain would likely become more severe as I grew and that my spleen might be enlarged. The doctor essentially instructed us to grin and bear it while watching for any problems that might occur.

When I returned from the Mayo Clinic I continued my active, little boy life. I played football with my friends. I broke my right leg, a consequence both of GD and of too little time allowed for healing from the biopsy.

I recovered and became a passionate sports participant, though I harbored little fondness for football. The experience of GD became remarkably consistent for me from this time until I turned fifteen.

I could expect that two or three times annually, usually coinciding with the changing weather patterns of spring and fall, I would endure episodes of severe pain in one of my knees, beginning with a slight swelling which would escalate until my knee looked like a softball, preventing any weight-bearing on that leg, and causing constant excruciating pain. These episodes usually lasted about two weeks before slowly subsiding until the last remaining vestiges of what we then called "attacks," but now label bone crises, disappeared.

At the age of fifteen I felt infrequent but consistent sharp pain in the groin area of my left hip. After an entire summer of visits to my doctor and no clues about the origin of this mysterious pain, an X-ray detected a healing, hairline, hip fracture.

My doctor warned me I could never again jump or run without risking another fracture. This devastated me.

In the past year or so I had just begun to blossom as an athlete whose dream to play right field for the Detroit Tigers' major league baseball team seemed plausible. I tested the soundness of his advice.

I contained myself during the long Michigan winter, but with the arrival of spring I resisted temptation no longer. I joined my friends celebrating the dawn of summer playing basketball and baseball games. I remember distinctly the thrill of getting a hit on the baseball diamond and the subsequent run to first base.

On my way to the coveted bag I knew I had rebroken my hip. I told no one. I meant to enjoy the remainder of this day, before any new reality intervened.

I saw my doctor once again, and spent several subsequent months supporting my rebroken hip walking with crutches. This time the doctor sternly admonished me that if I attempted such foolishness again a hospital stay would be necessary and I would require bone grafts.

I grudgingly absorbed this information. I began to transfer my interest from involvement in athletics to writing. I began to respond to feelings, both positive and negative, in the only way I knew: I wrote about them.

I got through the remainder of my high school years with the thought of leaving home, entering college, and pursuing a career. During my initial year of higher education at Southern Illinois University in Carbondale (chosen largely because of its location and warm climate, compared to the rest of Illinois, where my parents had recently moved, and our belief that such a climate would improve my health) I experienced severe pains in my left hip.

My doctor decided I should now wear a full-length hip brace to alleviate weight and pressure on my hip. I wore the brace for a year-and-a-half. Then I transferred to the University of Arizona in Tucson, again prompted to try the renowned climate for health reasons. A new physician felt I should abandon the brace because it would lead to the atrophy of my leg muscles. I took his advice and happily relinquished the brace. Although I did experience some pain, it was not enough to prevent me from enjoying long walks, one of my favorite pastimes, without too much discomfort.

These were incredibly happy times. I loved Arizona, enjoyed the climate that stayed consistently warm year-round, pursued my studies with enthusiasm, met many wonderful people, and fell in love.

Until 1974, when I was twenty-two, I experienced no bone crises in the sunny Tucson atmosphere. My first episode of great pain occurred in the summer immediately following my marriage. I did not realize at the time how greatly an emotional change, such as matrimony, could adversely affect my health, but in retrospect, I am aware that alterations in my emotional atmosphere can be just as devastating as the turbulence caused by weather changes. This particular bone crisis differed from previous experiences—the pain was not as great but it lasted much longer than any previous episode.

While this latest bone crisis still lingered, my wife and I moved to Las Cruces, New Mexico, where I pursued a Master's degree in history. During the two years we lived in Las Cruces only one bone crisis occurred. I did not pay a great deal of attention to GD, with one exception. My doctor decided to prescribe Demerol in an attempt to alleviate what by now had become almost constant pain. This became the first drug I used that actually controlled the pain I felt. I was ecstatic.

After obtaining my Master's degree, we moved to Norman, Oklahoma, in 1976. I began a doctoral program in history at the University of Oklahoma (OU).

While I lived in Norman GD affected me in many more ways than ever before-physically, emotionally, spiritually, and professionally. A year after moving to Norman, and three years after our wedding, my wife and I were eager to start a family.

I had long ago concluded that I could not bring into this world a baby who might have GD. My attitude today, with advances in knowledge about disability and medicine and ethics might be different, but at that time I did not believe I could knowingly contribute to the birth of an infant who might live with the severe pain I'd endured throughout my life. Fortunately, several hospitals around the country had perfected a genetic test, which could determine if someone carried the GD gene.

I knew that since I had GD any child I helped conceive would harbor the gene, but I also knew that a carrier did not necessarily have the disease itself. The question remained if my spouse carried the gene. We planned a 1977 vacation largely around the opportunity to go to Chicago to take the genetic test.

My wife was not a carrier. We thrilled to the prospect of beginning a family. In the summer of 1978, our daughter, Aimee, arrived.

I quickly learned that a person with weak hips and knees did not have an easy time caring for a growing infant. Although I wished to contribute equally to the care of my daughter, I discovered certain activities, such as carrying her, did not fit well with the way GD affected me. Despite my love of children, I rapidly decided that the requirements of an infant were not geared to my body and that one child would be enough.

Looking back I understand that I did not have to walk around carrying my child. Alternatives existed. Knowledge of those possibilities, however, still lay in my future.

When we moved to Norman I found an orthopedic physician, which I did whenever I moved. I also sought a hematologist. In New Mexico I'd been warned that GD could affect my internal health and that my blood should be periodically monitored.

My new bone doctor declared that my hips deteriorated so much that one day I'd want hip replacements. He cautioned me to delay such an operation as long as possible. That way I could take advantage of new medical technology. Since hip replacements did not last a lifetime, the longer a patient waits for the surgery the more likely our artificial limbs will outlast us.

I asked my doctor about using a wheelchair while awaiting hip replacements. He advised me to avoid wheelchairs because once people use wheelchairs they never seem to get away from them.

While I waited for my doctor to decide when to replace my hips, I'd started to see a hematologist. She became concerned about my white blood and platelet counts and my rapidly growing spleen.

Research about GD in the 1970s led to new discoveries about the disease, including its cause. GD occurs because our bodies do not make enough of a particular enzyme, called glucocerebrosidase, to eliminate it from our systems.

In a person with GD, these cells that are not eliminated most commonly accumulate in organs such as the spleen and liver, and in bones. Several strains of GD are known. One type is fatal, usually at an early (pre-teen) age. A second type causes onset of central nervous system problems, usually later in life. The type I have, labeled Type 1, is progressive, but not fatal. The earlier in life it manifests itself the more likely an individual is to experience GD related problems.

In my case, these excess GD cells caused my bone problems. They'd weakened my bones so that breakages happened easily. As the fatty cells continued to be produced by my body they accumulated in my spleen. Although the spleen resides in the lower left half of the torso, mine had gotten so big it began to look like I might be pregnant. My hematologist carefully monitored my spleen size and blood counts while learning as much as she could about GD.

If the spleen had only been absorbing GD cells, my hematologist might not have worried. But my spleen also seemed to be taking in many platelets and white blood cells. My doctor stated that my platelet and white blood counts were so low I should be sick all the time. I wasn't.

Except for GD bone pain I rarely felt ill. My doctor consulted books and other physicians. She found little to guide her. Some articles indicated if a GD patient lost their spleen, bone pain intensified. But most GD patients whose spleens became enlarged did so before adolescence. I was an unusual case, within the confines of an unusual disease. The best medical advice remained to remove the spleen and hope the platelet and white counts returned to normal.

My hematologist also hoped that removal of my spleen might alleviate some of the more intense bone pain I had recently begun to experience. In the summer of 1979 I began to have a great deal of pain in my left ankle. No GD was diagnosed in the area, but the pain was real. I was advised to walk with a cane to absorb some of the pressure.

While these medical adventures continued, so did the rest of my life. My daughter continued to grow and provide much joy. My studies never ceased. In the spring of 1980 I began dissertation research.

I wrote about Henry James, Sr., a nineteenth century iconoclastic philosopher and theologian. James, Sr. is also known as the father of Henry, the well-known novelist, William, the renowned psychologist, and Alice, whose diary of undiagnosed aches and pains has become a model of the frustration that characterized middle and upper class nineteenth century women who could find no outlets for their intellect. The elder Henry James spent his adult life in the Cambridge, Massachusetts, area. I anticipated studying his papers at Harvard's Houghton Library. I visited Harvard for a week during the 1980 spring break and discovered a wealth of material. I planned a return trip.

I spent six weeks in the Cambridge area that summer. In many ways it was a wonderful time—I visited a library daily, explored the Boston area at nights and on weekends and waited anxiously for the last two weeks of my trip when my wife and daughter planned to join me. By the time my family arrived the pain in my ankles had increased enough for me to abandon my cane for crutches. Even with the aid of these devices it was difficult to walk.

When we returned to Oklahoma I kept using crutches for support, unable to go back to the use of a cane. Intense bone pain persisted. After one unusually long shopping trip I learned my walking caused a hairline fracture in my right hip. My doctor warned me about doing too much, reminding me that with my body I had to be cautious and pace myself.

I refused. Instead I used Demerol to allay the pain. My internal organ and blood counts superseded concern with any bone involvement.

I had a splenectomy in March 1981. My spleen weighed close to fourteen pounds, riddled with GD cells, and made an appearance in at least one medical textbook describing GD.

Two months later I earned a doctorate in United States Intellectual history. That good piece of news did not lead to the next one, which would be a job.

But I got lucky. The history department at OU attempted to help graduates who could not locate jobs by hiring one recent graduate a year to teach American history survey courses. I became the second person to fill this position.

While I still used crutches, I began seeking wheelchairs for trips that required walking long distances. I saw a new orthopedic physician in Oklahoma City who stated my right hip looked worse than any GD hip he'd ever observed. He too cautioned against a hip replacement until I could no longer stand the pain.

When I, in frustration at hearing this advice once more, asked what constituted too much pain I learned that the time for a hip replacement would be when I experienced so much discomfort that I could not sleep, even with medication. I concluded that stage had not yet occurred and continued with my daily routine. That routine now included daily doses of Ascriptin and Indocin, an anti-inflammatory drug, to prevent, hopefully, serious joint swelling, which seemed to be the cause not only of pain, but also of bone crises.

In the spring of 1981 I attended a party where I threw around a Frisbee and played softball, all while sitting in a chair. While enjoying these activities my back started to hurt. I assumed I pulled a muscle. But the pain did not subside.

I saw a doctor. No cause for the back pain could be determined. Then, reminiscent of how I first discovered I'd broken a hip, an X-ray revealed that I had broken a vertebra. By now the healing process had almost finished. In the future I had to take care not to strain my back.

While teaching history survey classes I made two new friends who changed my life. Both were students in one of my classes. After the first day, they came up to me and asked if they could tape my lectures. One of these students was blind. Another had a visual impairment. In an attempt to bond I told them I used a cane or crutches.

We did connect. We began to talk outside of class about subjects other than history. I learned about a new organization called the Independent Living Project (ILP) that advocated for the integration of people with disabilities in all aspects of life, including housing, transportation, and employment. The ILP encouraged individuals with disabilities to talk to one another about their life experiences and to help each other figure out how to live in a world designed for nondisabled people.

The ILP had Board openings. Would I be interested? I couldn't imagine wanting to add another meeting to my life, but to be polite I said I'd attend one.

I left that meeting amazed. Unlike most meetings I sat through, participants at this one accomplished something. The ILP planned a statewide conference to introduce people to its existence and to educate us about disability issues. I decided to join the Board.

I concluded my year of teaching at OU. No history job appeared. As I sat at home hoping for something to develop, I began to do some volunteer work at the ILP. Then one day, I got an exciting call.

A representative of an association based in Tulsa called the history department chair to ask if he could recommend anyone to write an organizational history. He suggested me. He gave me their phone number and I immediately called. I talked to an individual who encouraged me to write a proposal for a book. I did. He liked my narrative. But I knew nothing about budgets, so he helped me with that part. Over the phone, I got the job.

Not long after we came to a verbal agreement my new contact traveled to Oklahoma City. We met. I was as nervous as could be. That didn't seem to bother him. But my crutches did.

He wanted to know why I used crutches? He wanted to know all about my disability. I had no trouble sharing. This had been the pattern of my life.

We left one another with the understanding that he'd call me to set up a time to travel to Tulsa and finalize arrangements. The call never came.

After about a week of waiting I called my contact. He told me they'd changed their minds about me. They decided that since I used crutches I didn't have the stamina to do the job. In one statement he summarized their position. If I'd had the physique of a football player, then maybe I'd have the stamina to do the job, but since I was a skinny, unathletic looking guy, they didn't believe I could do the work required to write a book.

I slammed down the phone. I got in my car and drove to the ILP. I asked what I could do about this blatant discrimination. The answer I got was "nothing." I tried several other organizations and all said the same thing. I met with a lawyer who agreed that discrimination occurred, but that it was not illegal. I finally found myself at the state Human Rights Commission office. They listened to my complaint, did the appropriate paperwork, and agreed with the attorney. I'd been discriminated against because of my disability, but no law prevented that from happening.

I became radicalized overnight.

While I waited for the Human Rights Commission decision, I started going to the ILP every day and volunteering. At the end of summer I learned they would have two new positions funded in the fall. Would I be interested in applying for one? Definitely.

I started working at the ILP as an independent living specialist, providing consumer skills training, peer support, and developing community organizing. I worked there for one year before GD once again seriously affected my life. I refractured vertebrae in my back while making love with my wife. This exacerbated a strained marriage.

The break in my back did not heal normally as it had done the first time. Instead it became a serious medical episode and a watershed event in my life.

I lay in bed for two months, unable to tolerate the pain without generous doses of narcotics. Demerol became like candy. I ingested so much I am amazed I didn't overdose while sleeping off its effects. The drugs did not have their previous efficacy because of the constant, intense pain.

I managed to get to my orthopedic physician's office. He immediately consulted my hematologist. Together they recommended I see a neurosurgeon. I did. He wanted to perform a spinal myelogram to determine the damage to my back, but he did not insist on the procedure. I declined.

I decided I did not trust any physicians in the Oklahoma City area with the current status of my back. I knew that GD had become a priority for researchers at the National Institutes of Health (NIH) in Bethesda, Maryland. I wanted to see the best. I informed my hematologist that I wished to go to NIH. She arranged a trip there.

One day in the late winter of 1983 my wife and I flew to the east coast. Prior to the trip I experienced some paralysis in my legs. After the long trip and the ride from the airport to NIH no feeling in my legs remained, a lot of spasticity began, and I could not control the movement of my legs.

The NIH doctors declared their amazement that I survived the journey from Oklahoma to Maryland as well as I had. Then they examined me, sedated me, and put me to bed.

NIH performed a myelogram. It wasn't good news. They found at least two fractured vertebrae. But they did not have adequate facilities to provide me with appropriate attention.

They arranged my transfer to Massachusetts General Hospital in Boston as soon as they felt I could be moved. Mass General had expert orthopedic physicians and knew about GD. I would be helped there.

Within a few days we flew an air ambulance to Boston. I lay within the confines of the small plane for hours, strapped in a prone position, staring at the ceiling wondering what my future would hold. After a seemingly endless plane ride, I got into a conventional ambulance and rode to Mass General.

That hospital quickly admitted me, then poked and pinched and told me that I needed surgery as soon as some of my strength returned. Drugs were readministered.

I spent the next few days in a stupor. I remember waking only to watch episodes of *M*A*S*H* and to inquire about when the surgery would occur.

Before long the big day arrived. I went to the operating room. Cowbone was added to my bone to strengthen my vertebrae. Harrington rods, long steel columns, were installed. During the surgery itself an additional vertebrae was fractured and the rods used were a little longer than originally intended. I moved into intensive care.

At this point I should return to my family. As I've stated, my wife made this journey with me. My father traveled from Illinois to take care of our daughter. My mother and sister both planned to journey from Midwestern states to offer support. My brother, who lives in Israel, happened to be in New York and he came to see me. Although I was two thousand miles away from home, I enjoyed the company of my closest relatives, an invaluable boost to my morale.

The entire time I stayed in Mass General I received visitors. Family, friends, and even people I had never met, but who knew other members of my family, helped me survive this ordeal.

When I left intensive care I was taken to a room and placed on a Stryker bed. This device has straps to immobilize the entire body preventing movement, which might cause further injury.

Lying in that hospital bed, literally confined, except for some arm movement, looking at the same four walls day after day, hour after hour, knowing almost everything and everyone I loved and cared about were vast distances away, I wondered why my body punished me all my life.

I lay for many weeks in that bed. In that time I began to change. I reevaluated my life. I found some of my attitudes about living no longer rang true.

The more I looked at the flowers by my bedside the more they became a metaphor for all of life's beauty. My body, wracked with breaks and bruises, started to feel different to me. I thought about athletes who suffer injury after injury and still return to the playing field. Then I realized that on a much different, and more crucial, battlefield, that of life, my body had performed amazing feats.

I started counting. A broken leg…numerous bone crises…a broken hip…a broken hip…walking for a year with a brace…bone crises…a broken hip…ankle problems…knee problems…joint problems…splenectomy…walking with a cane…walking with crutches…broken vertebrae…broken vertebrae…who knows what I forgot.

I lay in that hospital bed amid a slowly dawning realization. I began to smile—at me. I thought about what my body had been through. For years I despaired at my atrophying muscles and lost opportunities. Now I observed a body that had been tested over and over again—pushed to its limits on a daily basis—and survived. It was a good body.

I should not be contemptuous of my body. I should be proud.

Suddenly life became a gift, not a burden. For as long as I could remember I had thought of death as a welcome relief from the pain of this life. I was not suicidal. But I had not been overjoyed with being alive.

I felt that I'd lived a decent life. Whenever the Grim Reaper wanted me I would be pleased to go. That attitude changed. I realized that simple pleasures, like flowers by my bedside, helped me feel good about the world.

I realized that while I had achieved many of my lifetime goals I would never be able to accomplish everything I desired. I knew I wanted to see my little girl grow and become a beautiful young woman. Lying in that hospital bed, surrounded by pain, disability, and death, I came alive.

My metamorphosis is not unique. I have witnessed a similar process in many of my friends. When I altered my view of my body I also engaged in a revolutionary feeling about the rest of my life and about my disability.

I'd always perceived GD as an anchor weighing me down, preventing me from arising to my full capabilities. Lying in that hospital bed, I knew that much of my life had not only been affected by GD, it had also been enriched from the experiences I'd had because of it.

The people I know who deal well with their disabilities all have one experience in common. At some point in our lives each of us has come to the conclusion, not always consciously, that the results of our disability have been positive as well as negative. I believe that in our society this idea is an extremely difficult one to believe. We place so much emphasis on physical perfection that we refuse to believe anyone could benefit from a disability. But in my own case the evidence is irrefutable.

Disability provided me with a voice with which I could share my views of the world. I had wanted to write since I was a teenager. I had worked long and hard at perfecting a style. Disability rights gave me a context.

Lying in that hospital bed unable to move except for my arms, my mind traveled an eternity. I realized that my disability was the key to my becoming the person I wanted to be. My disability was the missing link to achieving my life's objectives.

Lying in that hospital bed unable to move was one of the best experiences I had ever had. I now not only believed in myself, I believed in this life. I wanted to experience more of it. I made a promise to myself while I lay in that bed. I pledged that from now on I was going to enjoy life and make the most of the gift of birth that had been given to me. Not only did my back recover while I lay immobile in the hospital bed, my spirit also recuperated.

I stayed at Mass General for about two months. The last couple of weeks I moved into a rehabilitation unit and for the first time in my life went to physical and occupational therapy. I learned more about my body there and continued to strengthen my spirit. When I returned to Oklahoma my body still needed time to heal, but my psyche had undergone a badly needed overhaul.

When I returned home I found that my wife wanted to separate. That discussion had occurred before, but I had never acknowledged her seriousness.

This time I did not consider her feelings much. When she stated she wanted to leave I told her to go.

This was a giant leap for me. I allowed my body to heal without having to interact with a partner. I focused only on the healing process I needed. And I did need to heal.

I came home wearing a brace that covered both sides of my torso from my neck to my hips. I had a fragile body that still required mending. I knew I would have to wear the brace for at least six months. Being able to deal with the physical pain and the emotional turmoil of this process in a solitary fashion was beneficial. When I felt pain I screamed. No one heard and no one was scared. When I got tired I lay down. When I was mentally exhausted I could work on my own healing. I was better off alone.

I was not so smart when it came to work. I returned to my office a week after coming back to Oklahoma. In retrospect I know this was much too soon. But I also know I would probably do the same thing again. I needed to know I was useful and to interact with my colleagues. But such a major surgery requires a long recuperative time. It probably took me a year before my body caught up with my activities.

That year was an eventful one. My wife and I decided to formalize our separation with divorce. My job ended in a dramatic fashion. Medical adventures continued.

An orthopedic surgeon closely monitored the healing of my vertebrae. My hematologist continued to watch my internal functionings. She did not like what she observed. Some thing still seemed askew.

I learned glands called parathyroids existed. Mine were hyperactive. My doctor wanted to remove some. I consented.

While learning about the operation my physician told me he knew no other instances of GD and parathyroidism. This appealed to my sense of the unusual.

When I went into the hospital for a parathyroidectomy I still used crutches. I hoped the surgery would do what the doctors wanted. It did. My internal activity stabilized. I also began to feel better. In fact there was such a dramatic health change after this operation that I soon stopped using crutches. For everyday activities I used no aid at all. No crutches, no cane. I still sought assistance for walking long distances, but not for anything else. Life indeed seemed like a bed of roses, but without the thorns.

During this period I suddenly became unemployed [See "The Walkout," page 25]. If this had happened in a previous period of my life I am convinced I would not have handled the situation with any dignity. Now I not only survived, I thrived. I believed in myself and I only continued to reinforce the commitment I had made to myself lying in that hospital bed.

I discovered I possessed the internal resources to live through a period of unemployment. After a few months I found a job in Oklahoma City, a twenty-five mile commute.

In the first week of work, in the fall of 1984, I wrecked my right knee. When my knee first started to hurt and swell I thought it was another bone crisis. After a few days the pattern of this pain did not fit. My knee had never been this swollen before.

I went to a doctor. He found broken bones in my knee and swelling resulting from internal bleeding. Minor arthroscopic surgery alleviated the swelling. I needed to stay off the knee so it would heal.

More important was the cause of the break. The stress of accelerating and braking in rush hour traffic had been too much for my weakened knee bones. To continue to work I had to adapt my car so I could make the long drive.

I needed hand controls so the pressure of driving would be taken off my knee. I needed to use a wheelchair so I kept weight off my knee. I needed some kind of device so I could get the wheelchair in and out of my car without lifting it and straining my still weakened back. I opted for a chairtopper, which looks like a luggage rack, and has a pulley-like device, which lifts a folded wheelchair into the compartment sitting on the top of a vehicle. Each of these devices worked. I used all of them for many years, including the wheelchair, which prevents me from continually rebreaking the bones in my knees.

Before my confinement in the hospital the thought of permanently using a wheelchair devastated me. With my newfound belief in the good life, resulting from my hospital stay, it was simply another adjustment to be made. In fact, it became not only necessary, but also positive.

Life was good. I sailed along in a job I liked. I shared custody of my daughter seeing her several times a week. I enjoyed recreational activities. I had many friends. I felt wonderful.

The first day of February 1985 was beautiful, sunny, and 70 degrees. My car needed a tune-up. I took it to a gas station about three blocks from my house. Since it was such a lovely day I decided to get my wheelchair and walk home. I started journeying on the sidewalk, looking at the trees and the activity around me. I neglected to observe the sidewalk under me. Within seconds I went from a lovely feeling to a sensational crash. Before I knew what happened my entire chair tipped over with me in it.

My reflexes have always been good. Without thought I stuck out my left arm to break the fall. It did. Unfortunately it also broke my left shoulder. For several months I wore an immobilizer unable to move my left arm. Between my legs and my right arm I was able to propel my wheelchair. But with a vulnerable knee and a useless left arm I could not drive. For the first time in my adult life I became dependent on other people for transportation. I had to work hard finding rides to work and back. I also had to depend on friends for rides around town. I became transportation dependent and learned first-hand what it was like for many people with disabilities when they simply wanted to leave their house. I became convinced that transportation, which had for years been an important issue to me, was the most crucial service needed by individuals with disabilities. A person cannot have a job, a home, a relationship, and make them all work if they cannot get from one place to another. My broken arm opened my eyes to this cruel reality in a personal way.

My arm healed after several months. Life moved along again at my desired pace for about a year. Then I rebroke the bone in my arm again. I became transportation dependent one more time.

I called friends for rides. I found ways to get to work.

I lived the life I chose.

HIDDEN TREASURE

[When I wrote this diary at the age of seventeen, I knew no one, nor did I know of anyone, with Gaucher Disease (GD). My family had always been informed that GD was an exceptionally rare disorder. I never expected to meet another person with GD.

I began considering writing as a career possibility soon after sports became forbidden. I chose to combine my interest in writing with the onset of a bone crisis. I didn't expect anyone else to do this. No one I knew could. None had GD or bone crises. I'm not sure if I thought I'd want to reflect on this experience in the future or if I thought I'd share it. I can't recall the exact motivation of those days in the late 1960s. I just know that something motivated me to write about the experience as it happened. I'm glad I did.

Thirty years later, in the 1990s, when I first began to speak openly about adjusting to constant, everyday pain, many people approached me to say they felt they'd received permission for the first time in their lives to talk about their own pain. In that context, this diary is not only the observations of an adolescent in pain, but a pioneering look at living in excruciating pain on a daily basis. In the 1980s, people with GD from around the country and then around the world began to connect with one another. That led to the publication of a slightly different version of this diary in the *Gaucher Disease Registry Newsletter*, (Oct.–Nov. 1984). The title refers to the lack of public discussion, at that time, about a person with a disability confronting how he deals with his difference and how this difference might be valued. Many aspects of the diary are painful to re-read, but I believe they accurately record my feelings of those days.]

December 17, 1968: I prepared for school. The pain became increasingly worse. I took two strong painkillers and stashed another two away for school. My thoughts raced back to Saturday when I was getting ready to go to a debate tournament. I took a bottle of painkillers. My parents noticed nothing until yesterday when my mother asked me if I was feeling well. Her curiosity was aroused when she found an empty bottle of painkillers in my wastebasket.

In the first two hours of school today I was all right but as I went into my third period class, the pain began to get worse, so I took one painkiller. I took the other an hour later during lunch.

For the next hour and one-half I was reasonably well. After that the pain hit me again. I asked some people for aspirin. No one had any so I lived with the pain until the next hour. When my last class started the pain was becoming unbearable. But, once again no one had any aspirin.

After school I was to be screened for membership in the National Forensics League, the high school speech honor society. Once there I again asked for aspirin, but this time ended up with Bufferin. I was thankful, although not for long, because it had little effect.

Tonight I was rather inactive although I tried to finish all the schoolwork I possibly could. My mother sets the breakfast table before she retires at night and she set my place, which is surprising because I think she believes, as I do, that it is unlikely I will go to school tomorrow.

December 19: It is a major effort to go from a laying down position to sitting up and much more painful to try to stand. When I want to sit I gently maneuver my leg from the couch onto the floor, with the rest of my body following. This is relatively simple and painless when compared to trying to stand. It is unbearable to put weight on my right leg, so I am using crutches. I take my crutches in my right hand and push with my left hand and leg. This sounds easy, but it's not. Usually when I have just managed to leave the couch, piercing pain runs through my joint. Every time I manage to stand, I am extremely grateful, especially since it hurts as much to be sitting as it does to try to stand… Today only one thing has annoyed me tremendously besides the pain and that is noise. The more noise I hear the more irritable I get, which makes life miserable for everyone else. Now, some painkillers and off to sleep—I hope.

December 21: Two things in particular have annoyed me today. One is when people turn on the television and I do not want it on. The other was that I could not go to the bathroom when I was up and wanted to. I think the only thing worse than not being able to go to the bathroom when you want to is going to the bathroom when you don't want to.

December 23: This morning was all right. But this afternoon I began to feel terrible. I couldn't stand the television noise. When the TV was not on, I heard it just as clearly…at 3:30 my mother turned on the TV. This was the last straw. I simply couldn't take it any longer and tried to fall asleep. My only words when I awoke were "Please, turn off the TV." My mother looked disgusted, as if she wondered who I was to order her around…

Today was somewhat of a milestone for me because for the first time since last Tuesday I managed to sit up. I could only sit for about 45 minutes and it was quite uncomfortable but I did do it. Once I have sat much of the battle is over.

December 25: [Being raised in a Jewish family this date did not have great significance for us.] My day today began at 3:30 p.m. That was when I finally awoke for longer than ten minutes. My mother said she believed I would sleep forever. I woke up many times before 3:30, but I wanted to be alone and every time I awoke people were near. I know it's not my family's fault that they are home, but I seem to be in a much better temperament when left to myself… My leg is not as bothersome as it was, but the knee and hip are still inflamed and still sore. When the effects of the pill begin to wear off I am in ferocious pain, but that is the only time. Tonight I shall see if I am well enough to sleep in my bed. This hide-a-bed has become tiresome. I told no one because I am afraid I will have to use the hide-a-bed tomorrow morning after I get up… My sister still has the flu and I did the best I could to keep her away. She *flu* away from me.

December 26: Today I awoke about 8:30 a.m., a normal time when I am healthy. I did not wake up during the night so I am going to sleep in my bed again… This afternoon everyone stayed home. My brother made a bitter comment about being in the house for so long (all morning). Naturally, I understand, but I have no sympathy for him. This afternoon, I played my first games since the last time I was sick. I barely beat my father at Scrabble, then clobbered my mother at gin. Of course, she came back and whipped me a couple of times.

Tonight I sat with my family at the dinner table. It wasn't as uncomfortable as I'd thought it would be. Sitting up can be very painful. As the day passed into night my leg was becoming more painful… Although I have had much pain I have moved around as much as possible. I am a disciple of the theory that if someone works a lame muscle it will soon work. It may be the most painful method, but it is the quickest, and I am a restless patient.

December 27: As I walked into the living room this morning I saw my mother converting the hide-a-bed to a couch once more. Now the only thing that is wrong in our house is me… I was terribly bored today. I am tired of TV and reading and sleeping, but I'm afraid there's nothing else to do.

December 28: This morning my dad once more went to work. For the first time in two weeks, I got up after he left. This morning I had my biggest breakfast since being sick. I had 1 orange and a cup of coffee. I was quite satisfied with it. Late this morning I went shopping with my mother. This involved getting dressed for the first time since the beginning of the illness. I have still not had a bath. We went to a nearby grocery and stayed only 20 minutes. But, to me, it was wonderful.

December 30: Tonight I went out for the first time since I have been sick… I did not have any pain all night. This was probably because I stayed in the same seat most of the night. Besides it was so good to see people again that I probably wouldn't have noticed pain anyway.

December 31: I get more liberal with my leg every minute. I often leave a crutch or both behind and try to make do. It is fun, but it can be very painful. Almost every time I do it I get sharp pains. Will they ever go away?

January 1, 1969: School tomorrow will be interesting. I once more will go back with a physical aid, a crutch. Not two crutches, but one. I finally decided today I could discard one. In a few days I'm sure the other will join it.

January 3: Today I went to school under my own power. It was not a brilliant idea. I began experiencing sharp pains so I began to limp, quite noticeably. I know I will not go back to the crutch though because it cannot be that bad, can it… After getting off the school bus, I took my longest walk in several weeks. Although my leg bothered me occasionally it did not worry me as much as slipping on the ice.

January 4: No pain.

HE KNOWS PAIN, LIKE ME

[My love of baseball appears a lot in my work. In this never before published piece I share one reason why.]

I listened every night to Ernie Harwell and George Kell describing my idols, the Detroit Tigers, playing baseball two hundred miles away. My grandfather and I bet a nickel on the games. I always bet on the Tigers. He never collected. I fell asleep listening to the radio broadcast of Tigers games on a nightly basis.

Playing radio quiz contests, I often won tickets to attend Tiger ballgames. Years later my father explained what this meant for the family. Trudging the entire family, my mother, sister, brother, father, and I to Detroit, watching the game, returning home late at night to face another day of school, work, or three kids at home. Exciting for me, hassles for others.

Grace. Al Kaline. The league's best right fielder. He eventually became a Hall-of-Famer who hit for a .300 average. I admired him more for his fielding.

Ernie or George on the radio describing the event. A ball hit to right field. A long ball sailing over Kaline's head and flying toward the seats. Kaline goes back, back, he's underneath it, he's climbing the wall, and he's in the stands. He caught the ball! But he's not getting up. Uh-oh. Looks like we may have lost him again.

Kaline broke bones just like me. It's the collarbone I remember. One of the few bones I've never broken. But Al did. He knew pain, just like me. He seemed shy, just like me. But, oh that grace. Just unlike me.

I wanted to be a ballplayer. I wanted to play right field. Just like Al. By the time he retired I'd be about the right age. I knew I wasn't that good. But I would be—just give me time. I'd grow into it. And I seemed to.

My body became more coordinated. My muscles grew. I began to hit the ball nearly as well as I played defense, which at times bordered on the spectacular, partly because it looked so easy, felt so free.

I thought about joining school sports teams. I'd be ready.

Then the pain came. My hip hurt so much I couldn't walk on it. Then I could. Then it hurt again. Months of living with alternating pain and then without pain.

No diagnosis.

Until the discovery…my hip was fractured, not a bad break, it just meant no weight on it for a while. No running or jumping. Ever again.

PART II
The Disability Rights Movement

THE WALKOUT

[After receiving a degree in history in 1981, a trade association decided I couldn't write a history of their organization because I used crutches. In the wake of this discrimination I found employment at a disability rights organization. In this job I learned a framework for understanding how my disability fit into a broader human rights movement picture. After I'd worked for two and one half years in this organization, I participated in a staff walkout. I wrote about why we did this in an article the *Disability Rag* (September 1985), published as two pieces: "The Walkout," and "Lessons I Will Remember." In preparing this book I realized that both my original manuscript and the published versions needed more context. I believe this remains an important, and hardly unique, story. This version includes extensive rewriting.]

I began my first day at the Independent Living Project (ILP) planning to study how to be an "independent living specialist," my new title. I intended to supervise the peer counseling and skills training programs. I hoped to transition into my new job. I knew I had lots to learn.

I could never have predicted how pivotal that initial Monday would be. I had no clue my first day could be so intense or confrontational.

I volunteered for the ILP about a year before I became an employee. I discovered a disability rights movement changing the landscape of how the United States, and the rest of world, viewed disability.

A belief about disability known as the "medical model" prevailed for decades, maybe centuries. We called this attitude the "medical model" because it viewed disability primarily through the lenses of the medical profession. Doctors and other health care professionals learned that people with disabilities "suffered" from conditions that required either repair, such as broken bones, or cure, such as finding ways to eliminate Muscular Dystrophy.

The disability rights movement turned this perception around and introduced new paradigms. Some of these new ways of thinking have been called the "rehabilitation model," the "disability rights model," the "social movement model," and the "disability pride/culture model." All share one commonality. They perceive disability as a long-term condition that does not need to be fixed. Many of these models propose that the changes needed are not internal, as in changing the person with the disability, but external, changing the environment in which we live so that individuals with disabilities can more easily maneuver through our society.

Just because we have a disability does not mean that we "suffer" or are "victims." We live life differently, not necessarily any better or any worse than anyone else.

I knew none of these things my first day on the job. At the end of my first night I knew I needed to find out about these differing views.

The state of Oklahoma implemented a plan some years prior to my ever hearing about disability rights that made my first day a busy one. This state plan called for sheltered workshops to be built in many Oklahoma towns. Norman, our city, happened to be next on the list.

The ILP's Board of Directors, United Cerebral Palsy of Cleveland County (UCP-CC), supported the building of this sheltered workshop. My colleagues, teachers, and mentors, Helen Kutz, ILP Executive Director, and Suzette Dyer, Program Director, did not. A meeting to discuss the issue coincided with my first night as an employee of the ILP. Helen and Suzette thought we should all attend. We did.

I came away from this meeting completely confused. It sounded to me like sheltered workshops were segregated work settings. While I didn't know much about what this meant, I knew I hated segregation of any kind.

I also heard people at the meeting suggest integrated employment avenues to enhance work environments for individuals with disabilities. Someone mentioned Projects with Industry (PWI). I knew a little bit about PWI because my next-door neighbor worked for one in Oklahoma City, 25 miles to the north. I didn't know much about what he did, but I left that meeting determined to find out.

I also knew I needed to learn why my colleagues and my Board did not agree on lots of issues. I ascertained that the UCP-CC Board included many parents of individuals with disabilities; some professionals who worked mostly with kids with disabilities; some who shared both categories; and a few individuals with disabilities.

Many Board members sat on this Board to find ways to integrate their children into the community as they grew into adolescence and adulthood. Early in 1981, UCP-CC decided to apply for 202 Housing and Urban Development

(HUD) funding. This would enable them to construct an accessible housing complex where people with disabilities, including their children, could reside.

Helen Kutz, a quadriplegic, who had been instrumental in changes making the University of Oklahoma more accessible, served on the Board. She cautioned UCP-CC about developing any kind of housing without providing services for residents. A disability rights advocate, Helen knew about independent living centers springing up around the country.

The name, independent living centers, made these programs sound like housing complexes. That was not the case. Independent living centers usually received just enough funding to rent small office space. Staff of these programs led advocacy efforts and provided services designed to achieve full integration of people with disabilities in their communities.

Helen knew independent living funds were available. She suggested UCP-CC write a grant application to get them. The Board agreed. Helen, the most knowledgeable person about this money, wrote the proposal.

The grant application succeeded. UCP-CC received funds to provide independent living services. In September 1981, the Cleveland County Independent Living Project (ILP) opened its doors. Helen became ILP Director.

When she wrote the grant application, Helen refused to call the program an Independent Living Center, the preferred jargon, because the UCP-CC Board did not come even close to consisting of a majority of individuals with disabilities. In the late 1970s and early 1980s, this demographic standard, labeled "consumer control," became the way people with disabilities judged the actual control they possessed of independent living programs.

Despite the UCP-CC Board's lack of consumer control, Helen insisted a majority of her staff, like herself, would have disabilities and would promote activist independent living concepts. Therein lay the crux of controversy.

Against this backdrop of philosophical (and some personality) conflicts I began my first day, which led to my being immediately thrown into a fight between the Board and my fellow staff members over sheltered workshops. Helen and Suzette opposed sheltered workshops because they employed disabled people in segregated settings and because those who worked in them usually received piecemeal payments most people would not even consider wages. Many times the workshops made lots of money for the people running them, but not the people working in them. The UCP-CC Board supported the idea of a sheltered workshop partly because they feared no one else would hire their children or clients.

A skill I brought with me to the ILP was research. I offered to discuss the situation with my next-door neighbor and to lead research about various employment programs. While we did this we also fought the state's agenda to put a sheltered workshop in our community.

The ILP had been in business a year prior to my joining the staff. In that time the staff radiated friendliness and courtesy. Many "consumers," jargon meant to convey that independent living centers provided services that people wanted to consume, considered the ILP office a "home away from home." During that first year Helen and Suzette tirelessly promoted ideals and concepts of independent living and the significance of mainstreaming individuals with disabilities into patterns of everyday, ordinary life. This is why the idea of a sheltered workshop seemed not only like a terrible idea, but a slap in the face of a year's accomplishments.

In my research about employment programs I became impressed with Projects with Industry (PWI) over all others for the simple reason that they claimed a much higher success rate of finding employment for people with disabilities *and of* retaining them in their jobs.

About the same time I presented my findings to the remainder of the six person staff, we learned that grant funds would be available to begin new PWI programs. We took the information we'd gathered to the UCP-CC Board and suggested we write a grant proposal for a PWI that they could operate. They didn't like the idea. They also informed us we could not use ILP time to write a PWI grant.

We did not give up. We felt getting a PWI into Norman of utmost importance at that time. So we volunteered our time and wrote a grant submitted through a volunteer organization called the Norman Alliance of Citizens with Disabilities.

We received the funding, making this the first PWI grant in the entire country operated by an organization that fit the definition of "consumer control." This is one example of the work the ILP did from 1981 until we walked out.

Other activities included:

- Bringing together, for the first time in Norman, a cohesive group of disabled people in a non-academic setting

- Working to implement a Medicaid Waiver in Oklahoma, which if successful would have provided services for people with disabilities outside of nursing homes

- Bringing $10,000 of Community Development Block Grant monies into a housing rehabilitation program

- Producing a cable television show and a national newsletter;

- Beginning a personal care assistant referral program
- Developing an information and referral database used statewide
- Working in concert with other service agencies throughout Oklahoma
- Holding two annual workshops, the latter featuring nationally renowned activists Frank Bowe and Judy Heumann
- Sponsoring an Access Advisory Team that advised area merchants about accessibility and hospitality for people with disabilities
- Expanding two programs into Oklahoma City, the State's largest community, that did not have any independent living services
- Sponsoring two peer counseling workshops, which trained twenty peer counselors in three different counties
- Providing the impetus for the development of the Norman Transportation Association for Persons with Disabilities, which ran a paratransit van, and
- Serving more than two hundred clients.

It seemed our efforts paid off in a big way. How did it go so wrong?

We refused to participate in the United Cerebral Palsy telethon. We believed this telethon portrayed disabled citizens in a degrading and self-pitying way. We advocated developing public housing in individual duplexes, instead of high rises or congregate housing, examples we thought of as disability ghettos. We refused to streamline our services to meet the needs of twenty-four community residents, who had ties to the UCP-CC Board, rather than addressing the concerns of the hundreds and thousands of other citizens who needed our services. We demanded service-oriented programs for individuals with disabilities, like the ILP, have Boards with a majority of knowledgeable disabled citizens.

We promoted what we believed were concepts of independent living. While we worked as hard as we knew how to advocate integration of individuals with disabilities into all aspects of society, we felt the UCP-CC Board continued to promote segregationist activities. The Board did not take kindly to our refusal to participate in their telethon and other activities they felt made life better for themselves and their families and clients.

All these differences surfaced into policy conflicts late in 1983. One precipitator occurred when UCP-CC hired someone as a part-time Director. This person seemed to usurp, with the Board's approval, the role of ILP Director. We did not react well to this turf battle.

We all revered Helen as our mentor and leader. None of us respected the person UCP hired, who it seemed to us acquired her job for all the wrong reasons and none of the right ones. What we perceived as micromanagement became a daily part of our lives. As people paid to rebel, this is exactly how we reacted. Then this UCP-CC power play exploded into what we considered a takeover of the ILP in early 1984.

The UCP-CC issued dictums that ILP staff use our time and equipment to answer UCP-CC phone calls in the absence of the part-time UCP-CC Director. In a time prior to voice mail services, this meant running to another office or programming calls into the ILP phone system. Ms. Kutz protested, taking the matter to her superiors in Dallas, who ruled such an answering service constituted improper use of grant funds. But the issue did not die. It was, in fact, the "straw that broke the camel's back." Or, in this case, the alleged insubordination that resulted in massive organizational change dictated by the UCP-CC Board, without consultation of either the federal government or the consumers that UCP-CC maintained it existed to serve.

UCP-CC decided to implement organizational restructuring. We described it as a staff massacre.

The UCP-CC Director, the person none of us respected, became ILP Director. The Board then informed Helen she no longer retained fiscal or administrative responsibilities. UCP-CC tried to cut her off from the agency that funded the ILP. The Board instructed her not to make long distance calls and specifically not to call those she considered her superiors in the federal government in Washington, D.C.

Helen could no longer make major purchases or plan major travel. The ILP Secretary and Bookkeeper now reported directly to UCP. Two advisory Boards were abolished.

We reacted with outrage. Consumers we served were dismayed. We submitted an alternate proposal. One UCP-CC Board member literally tore it apart as a Board meeting proceeded. They placed Helen on probation, after two-and-one-half years in good standing.

During Helen's probation several reconciliation attempts occurred. Consumers of the Project's services formed a new group, Citizens for Independent Living, and offered to negotiate with UCP-CC to resolve the conflict. UCP-CC did not take this demonstration of good faith seriously until the group made known their intent to alert Washington, D.C. of improper use of grant funds and personnel.

This was not an idle threat. Once Washington had been notified, UCP-CC appointed a four-member committee to talk to four consumers.

Negotiating committees convened several times, all inconclusively. At one meeting, UCP-CC members questioned the resistance of the ILP to serving parents of children with disabilities. Consumers responded that the ILP worked with all who requested their services, but the ILP grant specified programs for people with disabilities, not parents of those individuals.

While meetings happened, daily events became more and more intolerable as we found our every move watched. At one point, someone from UCP-CC told us we had too much fun at our jobs to be effective. How can one respond to such an accusation?

One day in early April 1984 I returned from speaking at an elementary school to an almost empty office. A note on my desk requested I drive to Suzette's house for an emergency meeting. I did. We discussed how much the situation had deteriorated and what we wanted to do about it. We concluded we had only one option. We had to stage a staff walkout and take our story to anyone who would listen.

We returned to our offices, cleaned out our desks, and walked off our jobs. Only the part-time bookkeeper remained. Five other individuals walked out.

We didn't disappear. We emerged as the volunteer staff of Total Independent Living Today (TILT).

Several months prior to our walkout, sensing the oncoming split, we created our own organization, TILT. The day following the walkout, a sympathetic community organization donated office space. With no attempts at publicity former clients found us.

Acrimonious feelings between UCP-CC and former ILP staff ran rampant. UCP-CC accused us of stealing ILP property. ILP staff sued for payment for our final working days and accrued annual leave. [Many years later we discovered another consequence of this time—our withholding taxes were not reported.]

The U.S. Department of Education, ultimate authority for the grant, requested a national UCP representative investigate the controversy. She held meetings with UCP-CC staff, former ILP staff, and consumers.

We stated our conviction that core independent living beliefs, such as consumer control, mattered more than the investigation's outcome. Despite threats or anything else UCP-CC threw at us we intended to remain advocates for our principles.

The UCP-CC representative, listened, pondered, left. We never saw her report, but we learned she recommended the ILP grant be turned over to TILT.

That didn't happen.

The conflicts that led to the staff walkout and the creation of TILT followed a two-and-one-half year struggle. These events occurred in Norman, but they could have happened anywhere in the country.

This is a story of the independent living movement in action. This is also a tale of a movement in [r]evolution. The walkout happened locally, but the events of Norman, Oklahoma do not represent an isolated "family squabble." The walkout contains national import and lessons. I have learned from this experience and what I have learned might be beneficial for every individual in the midst of any struggle for human rights.

To be effective a movement must be led by its constituents. People with disabilities are the only logical group to lead a disability rights movement. Only someone who daily lives with a disability can possibly comprehend its experience. Only we can understand the magnitude of change required. This is not meant to exclude non-disabled individuals. It is meant to pave the way for knowledgeable, committed citizens with disabilities at the movement's forefront. Professionals and parents jealously guarding historic leading roles must make room for individuals with disabilities or be ousted. If they truly fear the power of individuals with disabilities, as UCP-CC seemed to, they cannot faithfully work toward the movement's success.

If we, as a group, demand that non-disabled advocates let us through to positions of responsibility and authority, then, we too, have duties to fulfill. We can be no more possessive and fearful than any other segment of our community. If we do not seek amelioration for everyone, then we work for no one.

◆   ◆   ◆

The story of "The Walkout" did not end in 1984. Determined to publicize our plight, we talked and wrote about what happened. The *Disability Rag*, the most radical disability publication of the time, published our story in an issue devoted to the relatively new topic of independent living. The National Council on Independent Living, a fairly new association of independent living centers, banned the Independent Living Project from joining. Neither action seemed to have a lot of impact on UCP-CC.

I continued to live in Norman. Each year on the anniversary of the walkout I published a polemic about the lack of consumer control at Norman's independent living center. This lasted for three years. Then a huge shift occurred.

Two Directors tried to run the independent living center after the walkout. Both attempted to direct a spin-off to a consumer-controlled organization. They tried to do this because UCP-CC voted to spin-off the ILP to a consumer-controlled organization in August 1985, about a year after our walkout, when it realized that the federal government planned to mandate consumer control.

The question then became what group could become the ILP's new host. No appropriate organization existed in the collective UCP-CC mind, so they decided to generate a new Board to govern the independent living grant.

The first attempt to relocate ILP sponsorship to a new group collapsed less than a month before the anticipated transfer. A search for a new Executive Director began. I decided it might be time to put my hat in the ring.

The same people I had walked out on three years earlier now hired me to direct the independent living program. My tenure commenced August 31, 1987.

A staff of unfamiliar faces guardedly awaited my arrival. A tentative Board watched to see if I had anything hidden in my agenda.

Progressive Independence (PI), a name coined six months prior to my hire, became the second attempt to fulfill UCP-CC's now fervent desire to move the independent living center to a consumer-controlled Board before the federal mandate for "consumer control" became law.

Collaboration between the UCP-CC Board and myself resulted in the approval of three PI Board members and an officially incorporated consumer-controlled Board. Within a year the PI Board grew to nine members and received control of the Center on October 1, 1988.

I believe the walkout was the right thing to do.

Some issues defy compromise.

Two years after my hiring services and advocacy expanded exponentially. A consumer list that had stagnated to about twenty grew to well over two hundred. Our advocacy efforts became known nationwide.

This walkout remains pertinent today, twenty years after it happened. The kind of oppression we fought still occurs. As I prepare this book for publication, advocates fight similar battles throughout the state of Indiana, as well as elsewhere.

The story of Progressive Independence is a tale of success: success for those of us who were willing to lay our jobs on the line for the principle of consumer control we held too precious to abandon; success for the organization which bore the brunt of attack and changed its way of thinking; and, most importantly, success for the area's citizens with disabilities, our families and friends, who once again, after a lengthy struggle, found appropriate representation in an advocacy-oriented independent living center.

The walkout is only one story in the drama of people with disabilities attaining equality. It is symbolic of our movement and of the universal battles of oppressed peoples. Tyranny prevails on many levels, including bureaucratic and organizational ones. We must continue to be vigilant in our quest for freedom.

THE TRUTH ABOUT
TELETHONS

[I loathe every kind of telethon, including the PBS ones. I explored this passionate reaction in a 1985 newsletter of the Oklahoma Coalition of Citizens with Disabilities (OCCD).]

Recently, I chanced upon an article in *DISABLED USA* describing the efforts of a person with Multiple Sclerosis first to retain her well-paying job, then to find a new one that matched her abilities and expectations. She failed. Or, more properly, her society failed her. She unnerved prospective employers who were afraid her dreaded disease would frighten both co-workers and the public, not to mention render her unfit to be a productive, and compatible, employee. After several years of searching for appropriate employment she determined that her best route to continued success and continued productivity is through free-lance photography and other artistic endeavors.

Her disability did not force her out of the employment mainstream. Society's handicapping barriers did.

For several years now, I've been receiving the *Gaucher Disease Registry Newsletter*. I've even published articles in it addressing the importance of the disability movement. I was pleased to note that the *Newsletter*'s editor started to refer to "people with disabilities," and to include articles about disability rights and advocacy. But two issues ago, I was horrified to read two articles concerning a young Englishwoman with Gaucher Disease. She was constantly being described, and describing herself, as being victimized by this disease. I'm not going to maintain that Gaucher Disease is a welcome guest that should be greeted with hospitality. I'm much too familiar with its broken bones, heartaches, and physical pain. But I'm also unwilling to be labeled a victim who has survived its ravages. You see, "victim" has an ugly connotation that offends—no, enrages—me. Being told, or believing, I'm a victim places all the responsibility for the results of the disease in the disease itself. Now I ask you, does a disease feel; is it cognizant, does it manipulate? As far as I know, disease does none of these things, but people do. I resent

35

being called a victim because that implies that I have no control over the way I react to my disease, to my disability. But the fact is, I do have control. I can decide whether to succumb to my pain or to adapt myself to it. I can decide whether I want to grind my bones into pieces or to use a wheelchair for mobility. I can decide whether to risk passing this inherited disease onto my own natural children or to remain childless. I can decide. I am a victim only when I let my disease rule me. I am a person with a disability when I choose how to react to the characteristics of my disease. Anyone can choose to be a victim of anything. And anyone can choose not to be.

You're probably wondering, if you've been tenacious enough to read this far, what these thoughts have to do with telethons. Two things. First, I chose that title to grab your attention, just like telethons do. Second, it has occurred to me that the way the majority of us thinks and feels about disability has been shaped by telethons, by what we might call "the telethon mentality." When I think about Multiple Sclerosis, the first phrase that comes to me is "killer of young adults." When I think about Muscular Dystrophy, it is "Jerry's Kids."

Telethons may do some good. They may expose some people to disability. They may raise money for research and charity. They may give attention to people who need it. But they also isolate people with disabilities as victims, as subjects of charity, as a "thing" to be considered annually when their group's time comes to appear on TV.

While disability advocates continue to insist that we want to be integrated into a society organized to allow us access to all its avenues, telethons continue to segregate us as a population to be pitied, to be identified as distinct, and to be helped. The truth about telethons is that they are mechanisms of segregation. The truth about accessibility is that it is a mechanism of integration.

The point of this essay is that it is time for us to stop being victims. It is time for us to stop being ruled by our diseases, our impairments, our limitations. It is time for us to stop being ruled by our disabilities. It is time for us to control our lives, our environments, ourselves. It is time for us to control our disabilities. It is time for us to make telethons and "the telethon mentality" a thing of the past. It is time.

GENTLE, ANGRY PEOPLE

[*DISABLED USA* published this article in 1986. I worked at a statewide advocacy office, the Oklahoma Office of Handicapped Concerns. I still fought for a consumer controlled independent living program in Norman. And I became more convinced each day that people with disabilities could not obtain our freedom unless every other oppressed group also found liberation.]

Winter is not my favorite time of year. The cold causes my bones to ache; snow and ice are threats to my precarious mobility. But there is a part of the season I always welcome: the holidays. A time to pause and regroup. To contemplate previous successes and frustrations, to ponder future hopes. To receive gifts.

Four of the past five Hanukahs, the Festival of Lights celebrated by Jews about Christmas time, I've been given albums that evoke the holiday spirit. My benefactor happens to be a lesbian, part of another oppressed minority. From the start I've enjoyed the feminist music she's sent. I was immediately struck by the insistent, but usually not strident, tone of the lyrics on these albums. I was also impressed by the outstanding musicianship and inventive instrumental imagination displayed on these records.

One artist in particular, Holly Near, carried me away with her musical talent and penetrating social and historical commentary. Without doubt she first attracted me with her ability to sing about historical figures, bringing their spirit to life. Holly Near takes the journeys of Harriet Tubman (in a song composed by Walter Robinson) to a soaring crescendo and transposes this real-life hero of antebellum America's Underground Railroad into a symbol of leaders of oppressed peoples everywhere. By the time this song reaches its zenith I want nothing more than to join with all the Harriett Tubmans of the universe in their fight for freedom from injustice.

In another song, Near takes a quotation from the turn-of-the-twentieth-century iconoclastic, anarchist, Emma Goldman, and sings a joyous and arousing tribute based on the phrase, "If I can't dance, it's not my revolution." The message that rings loud and clear from this artist is that social change, though serious and vital, can also be uplifting. If Near were a mainstream artist, she'd be as popular as Springsteen or Wonder because she is just as talented and just as fun.

After I became enthralled with *Lifeline*, a live Holly Near album (which remains an excellent introduction to the Holly Near experience), I started to discuss her music with others. Few people recognized the name. But one friend both knew Near and shared my enthusiasm. In fact, she had attended a Near concert and related that not only was she a superb performer, but also used sign language interpreters. That snagged me forever. Not only did Near have a social conscience, but that awareness included disability.

A year has passed and once again the holidays are upon us. And, once again, my lesbian friend sent an album by a feminist artist. Her latest discovery is an Australian lady named Judy Small. Her vocal and instrumental styles are reminiscent of Judy Collins and she displays the social conscience I now anticipate from these artists. On Small's album, *Mothers, Daughters, Wives*, are poignant songs about sisterhood and senior citizens, along with dreams of nuclear disarmament, and images of beauty. And there in the midst of the album is a song about disability, about deafness. A song which strikes right at the heart of a disability sensibility. It is a beautiful ode:

SPEAKING HANDS, HEARING EYES

Jeffrey is just six years old, the biggest smile you ever saw
And there's so much I know he wants to say
But Jeffrey cannot speak to me in language I can understand
But oh the thoughts his fingers can convey

So I'm learning to speak with my hands
I'm learning how to hear with my eyes
So that I can understand what he wants to say to me

Sarah is my mother's age, the dignity shines from her face
There's so much about her life I'd like to learn
She tries to read my lips but I can see frustration in her eyes
And most of what she says I can't discern
So I'm learning to speak with my hands
I'm learning how to hear with my eyes
So that I can understand what she wants to say to me

I know she can't do it all my way
But if I meet her half way
There's no telling what good friends she and I could be

No cane in your hand, no chair identifies you
Silent and invisible your lives
So much to offer and our hearing world denies you
Seeing only handicap in the language of your signs

So I'm learning to speak with my hands
I'm learning how to hear with my eyes
So that I can understand what you want to say to me
I know we can't do it all my way
But if I meet you half way
There's no telling what good friends you and I could be
There's no telling what good friends you and I could be

This song is a touching exposition of disability awareness and a living example of coalition. Judy Small and Holly Near both embody a social conscience that includes a vast array of other minorities. People with disabilities are included in the cast of characters they describe and address. With recognition and inclusion of disability in their social struggle also comes responsibility. Our responsibility.

We disabled activists have a knack of talking coalition, but we are much less skillful at actually implementing it. Our rhetoric is all too often confounded by our actions. We are, at times, only too willing to neglect the rights and needs of other groups when we feel our own rights and needs are being threatened.

About a year ago I squirmed uncomfortably in a small chamber of the Oklahoma State Capitol while witnessing a legislative committee debate the merits of a Fair Housing Bill. People with disabilities were being considered as a protected class in this particular Bill. I attended that specific committee meeting on the slight chance that speakers from the audience be solicited.

I never got that opportunity. I thought that was a lucky break for everyone seeking the Bill's passage. I would have helped no one, because the longer I sat in that meeting the more frustrated and angry I became. As legislators dissected the Bill, it became increasingly apparent that the Fair Housing legislation was likely to succeed. But at what cost?

I sat enraged that a condition of the Bill's passage would be that gays and lesbians be excluded. I suffered through that meeting watching one oppressed group trade its rights for those of another minority. To make the entire situation descend even lower, in my estimation, I looked on while a gay colleague supported the Bill, as a part of his commitment to disability rights, while his own rights were being trampled upon. I watched in agony as my friend silently and almost anonymously endured without reprieve verbal abuse heaped upon the group to which he belonged.

Did this constitute a political victory? Probably. A victory for oppression? I cannot shake my doubts. I knew, abandoning that hallowed hall that I never again wanted to be bullied into any sort of negotiation that encouraged one group to obtain its rights by trading away the rights of others.

We, who profess coalition, also need to act responsibly. We have a duty to adhere to our rhetoric. If we express a belief in working with other groups to attain mutual rights, then no barriers should prevent us from working in concert.

The voice of coalition is a shaky one, difficult to maintain, hard to labor within. Despite its tenuous grip on our movement I still abide in the magic of coalition. I cling to my belief that working with other groups, both within and without our own movement, must persist. Not a single iota of skepticism lingers in my innermost recesses about the magnitude of coalition's promise. We can only hope to help ourselves if we are also in the business of promoting the rights of all other groups. If and when it again comes to pass that a disability group to which I belong demands our due at someone else's expense, then I, for one, want no part of it.

Some time ago my friend who shares my awe for Holly Near moved to another state. Dozens of her closest friends threw a party for her, choreographed by JustUs, a local disability theatre troupe. We included lots of her favorite music. The party concluded with a Holly Near song that delightfully combines joy and laughter with a sense of sureness awaiting the victories certain to arise from our sincere efforts to reform the world. Like the song about Harriett Tubman, "Singing For Our Lives," is celebratory:

SINGING FOR OUR LIVES

We are a gentle, angry people
And we are singing, singing for our lives

We are a land of many colors…
And we are singing, singing for our lives

We are an anti-nuclear people…
And we are singing, singing for our lives

We are young and old together…
And we are singing, singing for our lives

We are gay and straight together…
And we are singing, singing for our lives

We are a gentle, loving people…
And we are singing, singing for our lives

And I am a gentle, angry person who is writing for my life.

AMERICAN APARTHEID

[Progressive Independence, the independent living center where I served as Executive Director from 1987 to 1990, published this 1988 article in its newsletter, the *Advocate*. In a time prior to the passage of the Americans with Disabilities Act, many attempts were made to weaken existing legislation guaranteeing people with disabilities certain rights. This is both a response to one such threat and a general commentary on how society oppresses individuals with disabilities.]

If you use a wheelchair, as I do, you encounter daily barriers: steps; narrow doorways and aisles; high shelves; cars and buses unable to accommodate wheelchairs. If you are deaf, as is a member of the Progressive Independence (PI) staff, you encounter daily barriers: conversations; radio; television; music. If you are blind, as are friends of mine, you encounter daily barriers: education; printed materials; employment. If you have any type of disability, as do my friends and I, you encounter daily barriers.

Existing as an individual with a disability in this country is equivalent to encountering daily barriers. No other label than American apartheid accurately describes this pervasive, continual, and deliberate segregation.

We in Oklahoma recently held our Presidential primary election. Election time is always one of ambivalence for me. My polling place, you see, is not accessible to someone who uses a wheelchair. Through the years, Americans have been working diligently toward making the democratic process one in which all citizens may participate. But by holding an election in an inaccessible building, my county election board has, at the very least, passively endorsed voting segregation.

In my hometown of Norman, Oklahoma, a community considered the most progressive in the state by many Oklahomans, we have acquired a mass transit system over the past few years. Calling the system mass transit is, in a sense, a misnomer because it does not cover the entire city. But calling it anything but inaccessible for individuals using a wheelchair is a travesty. There are no wheelchair lifts on any of the buses. The system does provide a paratransit van for users who have a disability; therefore a segregated system remains the only choice for disabled Norman citizens.

In my daughter's nine years, I have frequently taken her to three day-care centers. Two are inaccessible. One of these day-care centers prides itself on its inventive approach and enthusiasm for multi-cultural attendees. No one with a mobility impairment, however, would be able to enroll in this day-care center.

A friend of mine recently returned to Norman from an out-of-state job. She asked us to find an accessible duplex or house. Several people, both within and without the office, spent considerable time looking for a suitable residence. We finally found one just days before she returned. No one knows how many accessible single-dwelling homes are available in Norman, but we do know there are not enough.

In the 1896 case of *Plessy v. Ferguson*, the United States Supreme Court ruled segregation inherently equal. This case applied to people with black skin color who wished to ride on railroad cars. Six decades later, in 1954, the Supreme Court in the well-known *Brown v. the Board of Education of Topeka, Kansas*, reversed this decision. This applied to individuals with black skin color attending integrated public schools. A lesser known-decision leading to *Brown v. Board* occurred in Oklahoma when another individual of black skin color sued the University of Oklahoma for admission to its law school. Few would dispute the wisdom of these more recent Supreme Court decisions. Segregation is inherently unequal. The view of South African racial apartheid is so negative that even a popular TV show like *Cosby's* is permitted to have on its set an "Abolish Apartheid" sign.

What about our own shame? Our own American Apartheid.

Progressive Independence and hundreds of other organizations throughout the country work daily to enhance the quality of life for disabled Americans. Regardless of how many solutions or ideas we propose, however, disabled people will never become fully participating Americans until America itself recognizes that its societal norms are denying us the opportunity to become fully participating citizens. In order to overcome American Apartheid, we must recognize it. Let's not mince words. Segregation exists in this country. Apartheid exists in this country. There is no virtue in disguising it. There *is* virtue in changing it.

Passage of the Civil Rights Restoration Act[1] would be a good start. But it is not enough. People with disabilities must become a legally protected class added to the more general Civil Rights Act. Polling places must become accessible. Building codes throughout the country should be revised and enforced to accommodate wheelchair-users. All buses should be required to have wheelchair lifts. All public places should be required to use Telecommunications Devices for the

Deaf (TDDs). All printed materials should be put on tape. Most importantly, for these and many other issues, cost should not be a stumbling block.

How do we put a price on human rights? Every human rights movement from time immemorial has been hit with the cost argument. It's a red herring. The untold cost in denying human beings the ability to be human is far greater than any other expense.

Abolish American Apartheid!

---

1.   The Supreme Court ruled in *Grove City College v. Bell*, to limit Federal agency non-discrimination requirements only to those parts of a recipient's operation that directly benefited from Federal assistance. Civil rights groups immediately protested this weakening of the law and advocated the passage of the Civil Rights Restoration Act of 1987, to include all programs and activities of Federal-aid recipients, subrecipients, and contractors. This statute clarified the intent of Congress as it relates to the scope of Title VI of the Civil Rights Act of 1964 and related nondiscrimination statutes. It was also seen as a precursor of the need to advocate for an Americans with Disabilities Act.

HOOKED ON SYMPTOMS: DRUG ABUSE FROM A DISABILITY PERSPECTIVE

[I wrote this article, published in *Independent Living* in 1990, at a time when almost no one in the disability rights community openly discussed issues of pain or addiction. When I wrote and talked about these issues in the early 1990s people identified me as an "expert," not because I was, but because so few others addressed these issues. Several organization have since evolved that address issues of disabilities and addictions.]

One day about five years ago I made a climactic decision. I would no longer use prescription narcotics. Demerol was my drug of choice, but I had ingested other prescription narcotics as well. I had recently been advised to use Flexiril, a muscle relaxant, for chronic back pain. Though no one could predict the ultimate impact of this suggestion the prescriptions for Flexiril became serendipitous. Consuming a couple of bottles of Flexiril over a period of months I began to notice a distinct personality transformation. The first day I took the drug I felt better, both physically and psychologically. The second day, though, I had a quick temper and low frustration level. The third day I would be moody and depressed. Stunned and concerned with my reaction to this drug I arrived at my decision. I would no longer permit myself to use prescription narcotics.

I knew that I would eventually want to chronicle my experiences as a non-drug user. But I felt I had to be careful not to analyze the situation prematurely. I gave myself a year. By then I thought I would know how my own "noble experiment" had endured. Those years, and several more, have now passed. What's the verdict?

For six months I touched no prescription narcotic. I had some withdrawal symptoms. I sweated. I was irritable. At times I craved a mellow feeling I no longer experienced. At this juncture I will state that I have no idea if I was "hooked" on prescription narcotics. I had, after all, been ingesting some sort of prescription painkiller for most of my life, since my first painful bone crisis, caused by Gaucher Disease, at the age of six.

An inherited, progressive, metabolic disorder, Gaucher Disease is the result of a low level of the enzyme, glucocerebrosidase. Since the body cannot eliminate all the glucocerebrosidase we produce it accumulates—frequently in bones and organs such as the spleen and liver. In bones the result is similar to arthritis, causing extremely painful, periodic inflammations known as bone crises. There are several different strains of Gaucher Disease, which know no cure. One type is fatal in early childhood. The chronic form, which I have, is not life threatening, but can cause extreme pain when associated with joint deterioration, brittle bones, and organ trauma.

The first two of the preceding symptoms especially affected me. There seemed to be no alternative to confront the intense pain that I periodically experienced except to take painkillers—prescription narcotics. My friends and relatives always expressed great admiration for my pain tolerance. But when the pain became unbearable, as it often does with Gaucher, I did not hesitate to call upon my painkilling friends.

The pattern of my lifetime had been one of determination to ignore my aches and pains. Every minute of every day there is pain somewhere. I would tolerate it as long as I could. But I am an active individual. I used, and abused, my body. When the pain interfered with performing daily activities I surrendered. I took painkillers. I did not believe I was addicted. I thought I could stop whenever I so desired. As it turned out I did quit "cold turkey." So I may never know whether I was addicted. But that is much less important to me than how I felt once I did quit.

When the last vestiges of my physical desire for painkillers vanished I noticed some changes. My thinking became clearer. I began to understand the term "in a fog" because I realized that I had emerged from one. I don't believe anyone else observed a distinction. I had been, and I remained, verbally coherent. The difference was internal. It was akin to tampering successfully with the fine-tuning of a television set. The picture in my head became a little more distinct, a bit better defined. I seemed somehow more synchronized to my environment.

In my newfound sensitivity I became aware of an ironic consequence of my decision to stop taking painkillers. I started having less pain. It slowly dawned on me that I had suddenly started to pay more attention to my body. When I experienced great pain I rested. I refused to rely on painkillers to stay active.

I also discovered substitute ways to help myself to feel better. I do not recommend my methods to anyone else. But I do relay them, because they have helped me to continue to remain free of prescription narcotics.

My first alternative is non-consumable, but often considered addictive. I have always loved TV. But I now ascertained that it had some physical benefits for me. Watching television is the only activity I do that keeps me still. Reading, which I also love, does not have the same effect. I move around. I get up and do housework. Sitting at the computer hurts my back. I have to pace myself and pay close attention to how many hours are too long. Since I do seem to require several daily hours of inactivity lest I feel poorly, I watch TV.

I have also become diet-conscious. I am unconcerned with weight loss because there is no need. But I have become extremely sensitive about how certain foods affect my health.

When I first sought to learn about controlling pain I enrolled in a stress management course. The most useful item I retain is that certain foods, such as bananas, contained an amino acid called Tryptophan which helps trigger the brain's production of endorphins, or natural morphine. I also discovered that other foods, notably chocolate, peanut butter and anchovies, contain androgens, which repress endorphin production. I began eating bananas. I found that if I consumed a banana a day I felt better. It may sound silly, but on days when I do not eat a banana I feel the difference. After several days I begin to notice more pain. Others may not be similarly affected, but I will continue eating bananas. I have since learned that L-Tryptophan is sold as an over-the-counter tablet that many people use to alleviate insomnia. (Since writing about L-Tryptophan, complaints by users caused the government to recall all brands permanently after discovering a potentially fatal problem in the manufacturing processes. My choice has been to concentrate more on paying attention to my body and using natural Tryptophan, such as that found in bananas and hot milk.)

After six months of no painkillers, my daily schedule became more compatible to the physical strains my body could stand. Then I fell and broke a bone near my shoulder. Did I take painkillers? You bet! My body had suffered a traumatic injury. This was not the everyday aches and pains which are always with me. Judgment is prudent in all aspects of life. I would have been foolish not to use a drug to lessen that pain.

After I broke my shoulder I periodically used prescription painkillers. But I never returned to my routine of several pills a week. In a way, I think I probably was addicted. I may have taken the pills just often enough to keep them in my system. I may very well have maintained a constant, though subtle, high.

No one—no doctors, no friends, no loved ones—can know when I experience pain intense enough to warrant prescription narcotics. Doctors realize the potential for pain therefore they will prescribe the drugs. Each individual must decide when to use pills to lessen the pain. I have been making that decision since I was a young teenager. Three decades of experience with prescription narcotics have convinced me that my own personal circumstances are not unique. They are symptomatic of a much larger social issue: How drugs are used in our society, particularly for someone with a chronic disabling condition like Gaucher Disease.

◆   ◆   ◆

Pain hurts. That's the best definition of pain I've encountered. No one likes to see someone else hurting. No one likes to live in pain. Inspired by compassion physicians invented methods to dull pain. Drugs are one of these methods. For an individual with a disability drugs might become an even more attractive option than for a non-disabled person. Drugs may do more than lessen the pain; they may also lessen the stresses of disability. Doctors are not trained to assist people to adapt to their disabling conditions, but they do know how to alleviate pain symptoms. So in attempts to aid their patients in confronting pain they may prescribe drugs. The drugs do have the desired effect of alleviating pain. They work by repressing feeling. If the only feeling the prescription narcotics dulled was pain they would be even more popular. But like other narcotics they affect other aspects of personality. When perceived as a source of personality alteration and as a means of last resort for physicians and as a method for someone to escape from the ramifications of a disability, then drugs can be the most pervasive, invidious problem a person with a disability can confront.

American television provides the most popular contemporaneous outlet for a fashionable anti-drug crusade. Television's war on drugs, however, is misleading. It is not a declaration of war against all drugs. It is, instead, a popular revolt against drugs deemed illegal or immoral—for example, smack, crack, pot, speed, coke, ecstasy, or ice. Movie stars, athletes, and politicians make anti-drug public service announcements. These public service announcements though, remain surrounded by commercials for over-the-counter drugs like aspirin or Excedrin and scores of beer, wine, and other alcohol advertisements.

While television's present crusade against drugs may be admirable, the kinds of illicit drugs that TV and movie personalities and sports figures commonly condemn are not the same drugs that individuals with disabilities confront daily. Prescription medicines, legal and easily obtainable, are too often the enemy of the man or woman who is disabled. Why then are "fashionable" drugs such as Demerol, Oxycontin, Valium, and other prescription narcotics so popular?

At least a portion of the answer to that query is deeply rooted in our social and cultural attitudes toward sickness and health, physicians and patients. Despite overwhelming evidence to the contrary conclusion—millions of Americans with chronic illnesses and disabilities—we, as a society, still insist on believing that medicine and doctors exist to provide cures. When a satisfactory resolution to an illness (meaning restoration of health) cannot be rendered—from a common cold to a spinal cord injury—doctors, patients, and families are frustrated. One frequent reaction is the inability to comprehend how heralded "modern medicine" can fail to eliminate their particular illness or injury. Physicians experience similar frustrations when forced to explain to their patients they simply do not possess all the knowledge necessary to cure a wide variety of human maladies.

When physicians are unable to provide cures both doctor and patient feel a desperate need to search for comfort in whatever means are available to curtail suffering. Too often the most obvious solution to lessen discomfort is to prescribe drugs. The person who aches from arthritic pain, for example, may be offered a painkiller to remove some of the hurt. The individual who has muscle spasms may be advised to seek relief with a muscle relaxant. And so on. The initial decision to use a prescription narcotic may result from excellent intentions on the part of the doctor, or healer, to allay some of the suffering experienced by a patient who has come to a physician for exactly that reason. A secondary and unfortunate reaction all too frequently is the vicious cycle of substituting artificial relief for pain while ignoring the body's signals warning the individual to slow down or find an alternative method to confronting pain.

The pattern of searching for relief from pain through pills rather than non-pharmaceutical alternatives is constantly reinforced by social habit and expectations. An individual with chronic pain who works an eight-hour day cannot afford to remain inactive when the pain intensifies. Many companies and managers still fear flexible working hours or working at home will be counter-productive. Frequent breaks or resting on a couch for a few minutes several times a day are viewed as poor working habits. Excessive absences are often interpreted as laziness, apathy, or worse, hypochondria. So the individual trying to maintain a career—or a family or attendance at school—seeks ways to continue functioning. Swallowing painkillers becomes more than an acceptable solution; it becomes so essential that the decision to kill pain with pills no longer feels like a choice.

Cultural attitudes about disability also enhance the likelihood that the pattern of ingesting painkillers will become the norm rather than the exception. How many times do we still hear, "I would rather be dead than crippled?" That's an incredible statement. Why is it that to imagine the loss of limb or sight or hearing is a fate worse than death? The primary reason is that we are so perfection-conscious that perceived flaws—particularly obvious ones like a wheelchair or a guide dog—seem to indicate failure to live up to our expectations of what is right. Making this perception even more dangerous is our American social and religious traditions of equating physical imperfections with immorality. Like it or not we remain ingrained with the belief that we have somehow earned our diseases or injuries. On the surface there may be disagreement, but our subconscious, collective feeling is that the person suffering from a disability deserves that punishment.

This sentiment, which may not be empirically possible to prove, but which I am convinced exists, is reflected in our environment. Even the most sensitive communities abound with physical barriers such as steps, curbs, and inaccessible transit systems. More subtle, and therefore more difficult to eliminate, are attitudinal barriers which lead people to fail to even consider taping materials for those who cannot read, whether due to blindness, visual impairment, learning disability, or illiteracy; or to attempt to integrate deaf individuals into the mainstream by mandating closed-captioning or providing telecommunications devices.

In my personal experience doctors continually advised me to do all I could to avoid using a wheelchair. Once I started to use the chair, I was told over and over again, the tendency would be never to get out of it. That attitude reflects the still pervasive belief that one of the worst choices an individual could make would be to use a wheelchair. Examine for a moment what that counsel meant to me. First, it reinforced my belief, as an individual raised in this society, that using a wheelchair was a poor choice while my legs retained any function at all. It was better, my doctors were telling me, to continue pulverizing my bones and to live with the resultant pain from that choice than to accept an alternative mode of mobility. Second, the pain that I did experience was great enough to keep me wanting to take painkillers—and to keep doctors prescribing them. Third, everyone I knew: physicians, family, and friends believed that painkillers were an appropriate method to relieve the stresses of disability. Of course, everyone believed that they meant the physical stresses, but did they really mean only those stresses? In my case, perhaps that is what was intended. I cannot know. But I do not believe that is uniformly the case. Too many drugs are prescribed to too many people for the cause to be physical pain alone. Painkillers can also submerge psychic problems.

Do not misunderstand me. I do not blame the physicians I trusted for their advice. There are good reasons not to use a wheelchair. One, in my case, is muscle atrophy. Other reasons, applicable to anyone, include architectural and transportation barriers. Considering only the disadvantages without understanding the benefits of using a wheelchair, however, is detrimental to all concerned.

Using a wheelchair—a vehicle little different than a car—for mobility reopened the world for me. Once again I could enjoy going shopping, without having to worry about rapid fatigue or pain. I could go places where people queued up in lines because while using my chair I no longer cared how a wait might affect my body. Once more I enjoyed going out with family and friends. When I returned from such activities after having used a wheelchair, I felt much fresher than when I tried the same activities with my legs. So I no longer needed to turn to painkillers every time I extended myself. For me, use of a wheelchair has meant both a greater capacity to participate in life and a healthier body with which to participate.

To the typically socialized American a wheelchair retains a vastly different meaning. It is a symbol of vulnerability—an unfortunate accident or tragic mutation—which is to be avoided at all costs. To the person with a disability, who has been socialized equally well, a wheelchair often becomes a daily reminder of a body indelibly altered and of new and numerous barriers. So the pattern and willingness to mask the pain of disability with prescription painkillers continues unabated and uncontested.

Painkillers can be used to enable an individual with a disability to remain content with their station in life, whatever that may be. A famous fictional example of the use of drugs to maintain stability comes from the evil Nurse Ratched in Ken Kesey's *One Flew Over The Cuckoo's Nest*. In the institutional setting of this story drugs are used to provide tranquility in a psychiatric ward. Another consequence of this policy, in reality as well as in fiction, is denial of routine activities and depletion of the social and human resources contained within each drugged and doped citizen.

What, then, can Americans do to prevent this tragic waste of human potential? To start, physicians might be instructed during their long years of education about the benefits resulting from the decision to accept the reality of a disabling condition—the use of a wheelchair instead of walking with pain, for example—rather than being trained primarily to seek cures. When the search for a cure fails, as it so often does, the alternative of relieving the discomfort of a disability with prescription narcotics is a relatively simple and uninspired substitute for investigating ways in which pain symptoms might be alleviated without pharmaceutical aids.

Doctors are singled out in this essay because as a group they are extremely prominent in interacting with great numbers of individuals with disabilities. But they are not unique. Medical personnel cannot be expected to become pioneers in social attitude. They merely reflect the assimilated perceptions of society in general. Doctors cannot be retrained in a vacuum. All of society must be reeducated about disability.

Few individuals recognize that disability in and of itself is not a completely tragic situation. Disabling conditions may affect the way a person accomplishes daily activities, but they do not eliminate the unique personality of each individual human being. People with disabilities are husbands and wives, parents, doctors, attorneys, athletes, janitors, and construction workers; we are healthy and ill; blondes and brunettes; loved and unloved; just like everyone else in all strata of society. In fact, disabling conditions place people in the most egalitarian minority extant. Disability knows no race, no class, no profession, no age. Anyone can become disabled at any time. Recent estimates indicate that as our population ages 40% of all Americans will be disabled by the year 2030. Teaching people ways to adapt to disabling conditions is not only humane; it is the only logical course.

Prescribing drugs to comfort those with disabilities may lead to a nation of zombies. At best, society will spend lots of money for prescriptions. Whether the individual with a disability, insurance companies, or the government foots the bill, costs will be significant.

Drugs are not inherently evil. Discrimination by both physicians and patients is absolutely essential to intelligent and beneficial use of drugs. But no matter how wonderful a drug is, particularly a prescription painkiller, the potential for addiction exists. Individuals hooked on prescription painkillers may not present a threat to rob, loot, or maim as heroin addicts sometimes do. But social losses are prevalent, especially in the person's inability to make the most of whatever gifts and talents they do possess. The temptation to blot out the physical, social, and environmental handicaps of disability by blocking the reality of daily existence is the most harmful and detrimental reaction to disability that a person can choose. The implications of the tendency to prescribe legal narcotics therefore are staggering. That is why drugs like prescription painkillers become the most insidious threat to the life of an individual with a disability. To enable people with disabilities to participate fully in the social mainstream, this form of drug abuse must be discouraged and eliminated. The devastating alternative is no less than the continued waste of human life.

THE SCIENTIST AND THE FROG:
A TALE OF TWO CREATURES IN THE FORM OF AN EXPERIMENTAL FABLE

[Autumn, 1991, brought a flurry of activity. We left our Oakland home only hours after a devestating firestorm narrowly missed our house. We traveled to New England, Oklahoma, and Kentucky. I also flew to Arkansas while Lil, my wife, rested in Oklahoma. I delivered several speeches on the road, which led to the next two essays. After giving an extemporaneous speech at a peer conference in Louisville, Kentucky, conference organizers requested a contribution to a book about the conference, *Peer Support Programs: To Promote Independent Living and Career Development of People with Disabilities*. I penned the following essay for inclusion in that publication.]

Once upon a time in a land where all ideas were considered worthy there lived a scientist fascinated by frogs. He liked little frogs and big frogs; spotted frogs and solid-colored frogs; baby frogs and older frogs; male frogs and female frogs. He just liked frogs.

The scientist sat around in his laboratory all day long and daydreamed about frogs. He wondered if they talked to one another. He wondered if they knew how lyrical they sounded when they croaked in unison. He wondered what it would feel like to be a frog? The more he thought about frogs the more determined he became to discover something new and useful about these creatures he so admired.

Eventually he formed a plan. He wished for nothing more than to test the jumping ability of frogs. How far could they jump? How high? What would they do if something happened and they were injured? What could he report about frogs and their jumping capacity?

He would not be content to watch frogs in the water and the swamp. He wanted to bring one special frog into the laboratory. Then he could experiment with how far the frog could jump under different conditions.

After days of searching he found his special frog. He was so excited that the very same day he took his notebook, his pencil, and his tape measure, and brought them and the frog to a long table. He took the frog, chattered with him, fondled him, and then sat him down and pushed, giving the command "jump" as he did so. The frog jumped almost the entire length of the table.

The scientist then measured the length of the jump and charted it carefully in his notebook. Being a scientist he wanted to test the frog in other ways besides this. He decided he wanted to see the frog jump as if the animal had done battle. So he amputated one of the frog's rear legs. He then took the frog, talked to him, petted him, and gave the "jump" command. Naturally, the frog's jump was not quite as long, and just as naturally the scientist dutifully recorded the jump in his notebook.

Over the next several days a pattern developed. The scientist amputated the frog's remaining rear leg and issued the command: "jump." The jump was shorter and its length was recorded in the notebook.

The scientist next had to amputate one of the frog's front legs. After he completed this task, he performed the now routine pattern of conversing and touching the frog prior to delivering the "jump" command. The frog jumped a little ways. The scientist recorded the data of the jump in his notebook of observations.

Finally, the scientist left the frog with no legs. One more experiment needed to be performed. He set the frog down, greeted and hugged him and issued the "jump" command. The frog did not move.

The scientist dutifully recorded in his book: "Upon amputation of all legs, frog appears to become deaf."

Do you recognize the frog? Perhaps it reminds you of someone you know or even of yourself? That poor frog, singled out as special, taken to a laboratory, and pushed around and torn apart, could easily be a metaphor for many a person with a disability caught in the cogs of an often abrasive social and human services system.

The scientist—the presumed expert—represents the malfunctioning system. His intentions may not be noble, but they are not malicious. He is simply doing what scientists do—taking an interesting idea and testing it to find results that he hopes will be of interest to him and of use to someone else.

This story of the frog and the scientist is not an exaggeration. Just ask any person whose disability is a result of, or has become worse because of, a doctor's, or other helping professional's, "care."

One writer described public stripping, a time when her doctors displayed her in an auditorium without clothes for the benefit of colleagues who could learn from seeing the extent of her disabilities. The writer wonders whether this is education or voyeurism?

Another woman tells the story of her father making casts for her when she was a baby and before she learned to talk. The doctor measured incorrectly and the casts did not fit well. The baby screamed. The doctor decided she was being a baby. She was. She protested in the only way she knew. She screamed. Agonizing months later the doctor and father discovered incorrect calibrations in cast measurements. The middle-aged adult still recalls feelings of helplessness and isolation while this medical "rehabilitation" continued.

These are not isolated stories. Many similar stories exist.

People with disabilities over the years have devised a number of ways to try and stop that scientist—or expert—from maiming the frog: us. One way is to get a bunch of frogs—people with disabilities—together. If we assemble in a group we invariably learn that we are the experts about many aspects of our own lives, for example how to pace ourselves so that our limited energy might last throughout a day of work and dealing with a variety of inaccessible situations. We are the appropriate ones to inform the scientists just how far we can jump—and about many other features of our own lives.

People band together to support one another. Because they are peers we call this interaction peer support.

My own primary interest in the past few years has been how groups of people coming together to provide one another with mutual support developed their own special commonalities—or culture. The story of the scientist and the frog is presented here in fairly tale style. The scientist could easily be considered a villain. The frog is a victim. But what if the last paragraph of the tale were changed to read in the following way:

Finally, the scientist left the frog with no legs. One more experiment needed to be performed. He set the frog down, greeted and hugged him and issued the "jump" command. The frog did not move.

He did not lie still either. Instead the frog's head expanded like a balloon about to explode. His eyes bulged, foam formed in his mouth, his body tensed, and his tongue grew to a length and a strength the scientist could not have imagined possible.

The tongue grew relentlessly inching toward the scientist. When the frog's tongue reached his tormenter it wrapped around the scientist until he choked the life from the bewildered man of science like a boa constrictor suffocating its dinner. Still the frog did not loosen his grip. The deflated scientist gasped his last breath, slumped to the ground, and expired.

The frog retrieved his tongue, crooned a lullaby, and then wrapped his tongue around the pencil. He found the scientist's notebook and dutifully recorded the following comment:

When hugged the scientist appears to lose interest in his experiment.

The entire fabric of the story has changed. The frog is no longer a victim. Why? Because he has done something that no one would have expected from a frog. He has done something extraordinary. He is now, in fact, a hero.

People with disabilities perform heroic activities, like the fabled frog, every day of our lives. In every community, someone with a disability is routinely doing something heroic, something out-of-the-ordinary. Because there are so many people who intersect our lives like the ill-fated scientist, where there are heroes there are also villains.

If, in our magical story, the frog sucked the life out of the scientist and left, someone would ponder the mysterious death for a while and then go on with the rest of their lives. Because he left a message there is more to ponder, but little else changed. What if the frog escaped the laboratory and returned to the swamp? What if he told his story to a group of frogs? What if they too had similar stories? They would be a peer support group, sharing stories of defiance and heroism.

I believe every person with a disability has hundreds of stories. I believe every person with a disability has at some time or another been a hero. I believe those stories are ones worth sharing. I believe stories of how we have survived, grown, and overthrown our oppressors are at the very heart of our lives and our movement. I believe that peer support must recognize the validity of the stories and bring them into the vanguard of our movement.

I believe the stories of our lives are the stuff of which myths are made. We have a tradition of powerlessness, oppression, and being subjected to savage treatment. But we also have a tradition of heroism, successful resistance, and survival.

We have stories to tell that would fill newspapers, magazines, and books. We have too often been timid in the telling-assuming no one would care or that we would damage our already fragile existence by parading our accomplishments to an unbelieving world.

In recent times a historian with a disability discovered a 1930s New York City group called the League of the Physically Handicapped.[1] They took their disgruntlement, at being excluded from New Deal programs designed to help people get jobs, to the streets. They established picket lines and sit-ins. Who remembered them? Virtually no one. They did not consider their story one that ought to be told. I vehemently disagree.

Telling our stories is the only way we will build our own traditions. It is the only way we will recognize the oppression we have been forced to suffer. It is the only way we will acknowledge the heroism that is delivering us from our enemies.

Peer support groups are perfect instruments for the passage of these stories. They are meant to provide role modeling.

Let's take our fables, our stories and make them into the kinds of myths that future generations will convey with pride when they discuss their ancestors-early heroes of the disability rights movement. Let's take our fables, our stories, and weave them into a cloth that enhances the very idea of peer support-using each other as role models for one another. I am convinced that each and every one of us at some time in our lives has been and continues to be that role model. We may not even be aware of anyone looking at us. But that does mean they are not there.

We have an obligation to set precedents for our children and our children's children. We have a responsibility to show what we have accomplished-and to share what remains to be done.

---

1.   Since this writing, the discoverers of the League of the Physically Handicapped have written about it in a variety of venues, most recently in Paul K. Longmore and David A. Goldberger, "The League of the Physically Handicapped and the Great Depression: A Case Study in the New Disability History," Journal of American History, 87(3) (December 2000), 888-922.

PART III
Disability Culture

I WAS BORN (IN A HOSPITAL BED)—WHEN I WAS THIRTY-ONE YEARS OLD

[I wrote this essay for a speech delivered at a regional conference in Little Rock, Arkansas on November 11, 1991. Attendees worked at and with independent living centers in Arkansas, Louisiana, Oklahoma, New Mexico, and Texas. A year earlier I'd left Oklahoma to become Training Director for the Research and Training Center on Public Policy in Independent Living at the World Institute on Disability.]

I was born in a hospital bed in Boston, Massachusetts when I was thirty-one years old—and had lain almost immobile for about a week. Most of the time I was drugged. It was the only way to escape the pain. A few days previously I had undergone major back surgery to repair broken vertebrae. My back was now supported with Harrington rods, two steel poles on either side of my spine, and an infusion of cowbone to supplement my own weak and crumbling spine. I was strapped onto a Stryker bed, a special bed designed to prevent movement of legs or torso, so I could not further injure my back. The only limbs I could use were parts of my arms. While there I blossomed into adulthood.

As I lay on that bed with little to do I gave my life a lot of thought. I focused on my body—that part of me which had gotten me in this predicament. I was tired of that body. It had given me twenty-five years of agony and I wondered how much more I could undergo.

In a sudden transformation people often label as a revelation I metamorphosized into a new person. My body no longer qualified as a temple of doom, but a sanctuary of life. I began a litany: broken leg; broken hip; broken hip; broken leg; broken hip; broken vertebrae; broken vertebrae; using a leg brace; using a crutch;

using a cane; using a wheelchair…and bone crises, with rebelling joints allowing no weight-bearing, sending chills of pain coursing throughout my body…

I was thirty-one years old and my body had borne more scars than most people feel in a lifetime twice as long. I thought about those heroes of my youth-athletes—and the dozens of times I heard commentators discuss the aches and pains they lived through. I realized that my body had taken an athlete's abuse over and over again and rebounded every time.

I began to view my body differently. For a long time it made me angry. The muscles I admired as a child atrophied more than I cared to acknowledge. The constant pain made me sullen. The sudden, sharp pains caused friends to look at me in wonderment when my mood seemed to shift without warning.

But the litany of breaks and bruises made me admit a different truth. My body weathered a storm of abuse—some of which was inherent in my being, and some of which I had heaped upon it in my rebellion against its limitations.

I decided right then and there to be nice to my body. In essence, I made a life-affirming decision. I recognized myself for who I was, with my disability and its limitations. I recognized myself for who I was, as well, with my disability and its affirmations.

A funny thing happened when I chose to like my body. I began to like myself. I embraced life.

For many years I believed that death would be a welcome release from the pain of life. But life no longer seemed to be unending pain. I took stock and found joy. I had a daughter I loved very much and it suddenly became very important to me to see her grow up. I had friends who were dear to me and I to them and I wanted to learn to know and love them better. I had a job that excited me and I wanted to continue to learn and grow in it. I had goals still not achieved and I wanted to stick around and see if I could make them happen.

I was born in a hospital in Boston, Massachusetts when I was thirty-one years old—and two thousand miles away from home. But home was very much a part of my maturation.

The job I liked so much was at the first independent living center to be funded in Oklahoma. That program, in Norman, is now known as Progressive Independence. At the time I served as Consumer Skills Coordinator, which meant I supervised and provided peer support and skills training. I also was a community organizer and editor of a bi-monthly newsletter. I had been part of the independent living movement for about a year-and-a-half.

My disability first manifested itself when I was six years old in the form of a painful and unexplained limp. After months of uncertainty I was diagnosed at the

Mayo Clinic in Minnesota with Gaucher Disease. At the time, in the late 1950s, the disease had been identified, but little was known about it or its consequences. My parents were advised to do everything they could to ensure that I lived a normal, non-institutionalized life.

I never went to a special school. I never did anything differently than my brother or my sister, or my peers. Except that once or twice every year when the spring and fall weather heralded a change in seasons I experienced the bone crises that laid me inert for a couple of weeks with debilitating pain and an inability to put weight on my legs.

A couple of weeks of missed school were a small price to pay to live with my family. I didn't know that then. I know that now.

When I was fifteen I broke my hip for the first time. My dreams of athletic prowess ended, though I was still unprepared for that reality. I continued to live a normal life, with my family, in school, preparing for college. The only difference was that I used crutches more often than I had previously. But that was a small price to pay to live with my family. I didn't know that then. I know that now.

I was born in a hospital in Boston, Massachusetts when I was thirty-one years old—and had already fathered a daughter. A wonderful, charming child who already felt the effects of my disability because I could not lift and hold her as often as either of us would have liked. A beautiful child. She had already traveled from Oklahoma to Boston when I conducted research on my dissertation in history. A vibrant child who had already felt the effects of my disability because I lay in a hospital in Boston, two thousand miles away from her when she was only four years old. But that was a small price to pay to be a part of my family. I didn't know that then. I know that now.

I was born in a hospital in Boston, Massachusetts when I was thirty-one years old—and just beginning my life's work. I began to consider myself a person with a disability, slightly, when it occurred to me that I could benefit from owning a disability parking placard. Why grind my bones walking further than necessary when I could get a card and park closer? I began to consider myself a person with a disability, slightly, when I would nod to this somewhat funny-looking lady who pushed the elevator buttons in the library with her cane. I began to consider myself a person with a disability, slightly more than slightly, when I began to use a cane to get around at all times and people started to ask me what was wrong. I began to consider myself a person with a disability, quite a little bit, when I began to borrow a wheelchair to get around in the mall, or the zoo, or anywhere there was a lot of walking and standing.

I was born in a hospital in Boston, Massachusetts when I was thirty-one years old—and a student of mine in a freshman history class introduced me to a new program in Norman called an independent living center. I began to know, and to like, and to identify with, people who used wheelchairs, people who couldn't see, and people who couldn't hear. I learned about a whole world of disability out there which I had never heard about and which I only began to realize I longed to be in. I learned that the big price I had paid for living in my normal family settings was that I didn't know there was anybody else out there like me—people with disabilities.

I was born in a hospital in Boston, Massachusetts when I was thirty-one years old—and had already been told that I could not write a book because I used crutches. I had completed my dissertation a couple of years earlier. I had spent a year teaching freshman history classes. I had published an article in a historical journal. But I was told that I did not have the stamina to write a book because I used crutches. Because I used crutches—and no longer had that athlete's body to which I had aspired in my youth—I was informed that I was not book-writing material.

My radicalism instantly crystallized when I felt the full force of employment discrimination because of my disability. I tried to fight my oppressor. But I discovered the law was on their side, not mine. I found that in Oklahoma, at that time, there was no protection for people with disabilities against employment discrimination.

When I tell this story today people shake their heads in amazement and disgust, then assume that the Americans with Disabilities Act now prevents this kind of blatant discrimination. It does not.

My oppressor, the individual who decided I could not write a book because I used crutches, could make the same decision today without consequence to himself or his organization. The Americans with Disabilities Act, like other anti-discrimination laws, does not apply to everyone. It does not touch, for example, employers with less than fifteen employees or those who do not receive federal funds to operate their programs. My oppressor would remain unscathed today for those reasons.

A few years ago I decided to transform this story of being told I could not write a book because I used crutches into an affirmation. Now I sometimes begin speeches by saying there is one person more than any other I wish to thank for the work that I do today. That person is the jerk who told me I could not write a book because I used crutches. Thanks to him, I analyzed the talents and skills that I have developed over the years. I focused on three skills that I believed I could do well: research, speak, and write. I decided I would use those skills to ensure, as best I could, that the kind of discrimination I encountered would never again occur.

For almost ten years now I have been engaged in this work. I have worked in an independent living center, a state office of advocacy for people with disabilities, and now the World Institute on Disability. More importantly, I have met people from around the world who tell stories similar to my own. I have traveled all around this nation, and expect in the future to travel around this world. I have been given the gift of combining my two loves—scholarly activities and human rights—into disability rights activism. I am being paid for doing what I would do for nothing, for what I believe in, and for what I must do because that is who I am. I have one person more than any other to thank for my success. The person who told me that I could not write a book because I used crutches.

I was born in a hospital in Boston, Massachusetts when I was thirty-one years old—and started to understand, in a way that I could not then define, that my disability had brought to me as many positive consequences as negative ones. A few years ago a friend commented to me that losing his leg was the best thing that had ever happened to him. I looked at him in amazement and wondered what he could possibly be thinking. He informed me that until his accident his life had never had focus. Because of his disability he had settled down and found a path. From that conversation I developed the following generalization: people I know who have adjusted well to their disability all have one trait in common—somewhere along the way they realized that as many positive results as negative ones had succeeded their disabling conditions. I have made this statement so many times now to other people with disabilities that I do not expect to be contradicted. Not once has someone disagreed with this generalization. In a way, I guess, this statement is now a self-fulfilling prophecy. I present it as an accomplished fact. Only someone bent on argument seems likely to challenge it. I may be wrong. There may be people with disabilities who are well adjusted and have not made this particular leap. I don't think it matters much anymore. Enough people agree with the statement that its truth is prevalent enough for my satisfaction.

I was born in a hospital in Boston, Massachusetts when I was thirty-one years old—and had no idea that in less than ten years the most important work I could do would be to tell and collect stories about what it is like to be a person with a disability in this world. I have told my version of the story of the birth of independent living in this country many times to many diverse audiences. How a group of people in Berkeley calling themselves the Rolling Quads lived in a hospital while they attended the University of California. How they got together and began talking to one another. They discovered that there was only one reason that they were living in that hospital: their society had no accommodations for them. They could not get around Berkeley because there were no curb cuts for them to roll on. They could not live in the community because no houses there were adapted for their needs. They feared going too far from their home base—the hospital—because if their wheelchairs happened to break down there were no repair services for them to call on.

Those Berkeley pioneers changed their community. They took tar and concrete and made their own makeshift ramps from the streets to the sidewalks. Those ramps still exist. In the past year I've used them myself. My friends in the Bay Area now all live in the community. There is enough adapted housing in the area to make this possible. And the disabled student services program, which they created, still runs a wheelchair repair service.

A funny thing happened in Berkeley when those students with disabilities spread their wings. People who lived in the community, but did not attend the University, approached them. Berkeley became one of the first cities in the world to fund a community program for independent living for people with disabilities. The idea rooted quickly across the country and around the world.

Today the Center for Independent Living in Berkeley (CIL) is still considered the model for independent living centers. People come from all over this country, and others, to learn from Berkeley, from CIL, and from other outgrowths of that community, such as DREDF, (the Disability Rights Education and Defense Fund), a legal rights advocacy organization and WID, (the World Institute on Disability), a public policy institute.

Several hundred independent living centers exist today in the United States—and more all over the world. They are funded through a variety of public and private sources. Our movement is a successful one. We have brought our issues to the public and we are changing the world. It is still far from a perfect world, but it is a better one for people with disabilities. As we all continue our work it will become better yet.

I was born in a hospital in Boston, Massachusetts when I was thirty-one years old—and had only an inkling why my stories might be ones worth telling. I have spent the majority of my time here relating my own very personal experiences. But they are far from unique tales. Each one of you has stories of a similar nature. Each one of you has lived lives of quiet, and sometimes not-so-quiet, heroism. Each one of you is a hero. Each one of you has provided this world with some kind of act of courage beyond the expected. That makes each one of you a hero.

Not too long ago I was reticent to admit I had any heroes. I thought we were all equal and to single out any one individual was an act of unwarranted egotism. Today I believe that it is act of unparalleled selfishness not to stake our claims to heroism. How can we move through this world, changing it so it meets our needs and the needs of every other person, without promoting our progress—and our setbacks?

In the last year I have become a promoter—a believer in the concept of creating a disability mythology. I have become a promoter of the belief that our stories are ones worth telling and retelling. I have become a promoter of the belief that unless we tell our stories we are doing a great disservice not only to our peers, but also to those who will follow us.

Mythology is an interesting concept. It is the story of heroes and villains; successes and defeats; epic struggles and daily pursuits. Our story is an epic one. We have fought against great odds to get where we are today. We have come out of institutions and battled people who believed that as invalids we were in-valid. We have proven, and we are still proving, that by our very existence we are worthy. We are worthy of life; worthy of education; worthy of employment; worthy of families; worthy of success, and worthy of failure; worthy of everything that this life has to offer.

One of the reasons for choosing myth to tell these stories is that it has a certain set of symbols, which can be understood by any one, in any society, and in any culture.

When I first discussed disability mythology I explained my notions to someone from Japan. In an instant he translated what I said to his own culture. I have had similar experiences with people from several other countries and from many people within our own society.

In my pursuit of creating a disability mythology I have chosen to focus first on heroes. I decided to do this for several reasons. First, in my own thinking about the concept of the existence of a disability culture heroes play an important role. Second, people everywhere can identify with heroes and heroism because we all know people who fit the category. Finally, I chose to focus on heroes because it is fun. It is affirming and enjoyable to reflect on individual lives and tell of their heroic acts.

I have so many heroes in this movement that I cannot begin to list them all. Two stories will suffice. First, is the tale of the man who traveled in his motorized wheelchair to see a movie at a local theater. There was no ramp. The theater management offered to lift him in his chair and take him inside. He agreed. This sequence in and of itself always astounds me a little because I imagine in the same circumstance that I would have stormed away from the theater. But he did not. He went in and enjoyed the movie. About a week later he returned with half-a-dozen other individuals, all of whom used heavy, motorized wheelchairs. The theater management lifted them all in. And shortly thereafter, having learned their lesson, they installed a ramp.

My second story concerns a lady who, like me, was told that she couldn't do a job. In her case she was informed that she could not teach in an elementary school because her wheelchair was a fire hazard. Like me, she found a lawyer to vent her story to. But unlike my situation, her lawyer believed they could win a discrimination suit. They filed one against the city's Board of Education. Before it could be heard, the parties agreed to an out-of-court settlement. She became a schoolteacher before she too turned to a life of disability rights activism. I wish I had known this when I was told I couldn't write a book because I used crutches. But I didn't. Because not enough of our stories have been told.

My guess is that each one of you has stories similar to the ones I just related. That is why it is so important that we take time from our everyday lives to tell our stories. So we can feel better about ourselves. So our children have a chance to tell different stories. This is a small price to pay to be part of the human family. I didn't know that when I lay in the hospital bed in Boston. I know that now.

My passion has become the creation of a disability mythology. I will not rest until I locate and relate as many stories as I'm able. I will not rest until my heroes—each of you—have begun to take your rightful place in the world. I will not rest until our stories join those of the other great traditional stories of the world. Because that is exactly where our stories and our lives belong. In a history of the world that recognizes the accomplishments, struggles, and lives of people with disabilities.

I was born in a hospital in Boston, Massachusetts when I was thirty-one years old—and I'm privileged to be alive still to share this story of becoming.

CREATING A DISABILITY MYTHOLOGY

[This is a revised version of a 1991 speech and essay published in 1992's *Independent Living: Preparing for the Twenty-first Century Conference Proceedings*, and later in the Winter 1992 *International Journal of Rehabilitation Research*. It was one of my first public forays into promoting the idea of a disability culture. I chose to open the door with a discussion of how the disability rights movement could be framed in terms of a mythological adventure.]

> "...the folk heroes of disability and chronic disease have not been the millions who came to terms with their problems but those few who were so successful that they passed: the polio victim who broke track records, the one-legged pitcher who played major league baseball, the great composer who was deaf, the famous singer who had a colostomy. They were all so successful that no one knew of their disability, and therein lay their glory." (Zola, 204)

To this list one might add President Franklin Delano Roosevelt (FDR), a paraplegic from polio; the conqueror, Alexander the Great, believed to have had epilepsy; and the world-renowned speaker, Helen Keller, who could not hear or see.

Too many people with disabilities have for too long tried to pass. Our success has been seen in the ways we overcame our disabilities, not in how we adapted or used our disabilities to forge ourselves. Franklin Delano Roosevelt used every means at his disposal to hide the extent and severity of his disability. Imagine how different society might be if he chose to share what he learned from having an adult-onset disability. He might have discussed how his disability impacted his daily life, his personality, and his presidency.

FDR may be a hero to some disability activists. Others of us know too much about his endeavors to hide his polio and its effects from us. We are reluctant to claim him, because he too often seemed unwilling to claim us. FDR believed voters could not move beyond equating disability with weakness and, therefore, political disaster for him.

Many of us with disabilities have been reluctant and ashamed to share what our disabilities have signified in our lives. We've often had good reasons. We have been shunned by our communities, forced into institutions by our families, and even killed by our leaders.

If we will not promote our virtues who will? There has been a long-term argument in the United States about what we call ourselves. Some activists view this as a debate of utmost importance, others a diversion from more vital issues. But if we do not know what to call ourselves how can we convey who we are?

When we wish to promote ourselves as a political force; when we want to fit into diverse social groupings; and when we gather in conferences and meetings where we have opportunities to celebrate our lives, we find ourselves forced to come to grips with who we are—both as individuals and as individuals with disabilities.

Whether every single person with a disability feels comfortable in being labeled as "disabled" is not at issue. Enough of us identify with our brothers and sisters with disabilities to relate to each other in a manner that sometimes reflects society; other times feels like community; and in the best of circumstances resembles family.

Like other groups who have been labeled from the outside and sought their own identity, we too search for definitions of disability culture. Language discussions represent corner pieces in the jigsaw puzzle of our beliefs about ourselves.

James Baldwin, the great black and gay American author, wrote in his 1972 book, *No Name in the Street*, "When I was young, for example, it was an insult to be called black. The blacks have now taken over this once pejorative term and made of it a rallying cry and a badge of honor and are teaching their children to be proud that they are black."

Establishing identity for those of us with disabilities is not an idle pastime. The late Irving Kenneth Zola, a sociologist and person with multiple disabilities, wrote a litany of successes, quoted at the beginning of this article, of people who in some way seemed to distance themselves from their disabilities. You might say that they, or at least the society in which they succeeded, discounted their disability. Their feats were viewed as ones of overcoming disability.

When we buy into the mainstream notion of success through overcoming we submit to an ideal that we cannot possibly maintain. No matter what we do, we remain disabled.

Baldwin observed that, "To be liberated from the stigma of blackness by embracing it is to cease, forever, one's interior argument and collaboration with the author's of one's degradation."

Living in a society that forces us to examine ourselves by inapplicable standards is a plight that all individuals with disabilities find. The very word, "disability," implies in some way a difference from the more positive word "ability." We all know people with disabilities who are both more and less capable in various endeavors than our nondisabled peers.

Some of us conclude we would rather change the world to adapt to us than continue fighting to fit into a nondisabled world. We advocate, among other goals, for streets and buildings to include ramps, curb cuts, and wide doors; interpreters to be available at public gatherings; print materials to be disseminated in a variety of accessible formats; and Personal Assistants to be available to help with routine tasks of daily living.

I suggest these changes do not go far enough. We must also embrace ourselves as we are with our disabilities, our varied needs, and our diverse strengths and weaknesses. To embrace ourselves as we know ourselves, with our disabilities.

I propose, in fact, even more. I wish to see us not only recognize our disabilities, but to celebrate them. To sing clearly and out loud our praises, our struggles, our failures, and our successes: our lives.

One means of declaring our indomitable spirit and strength is mythology. To take our lives, our daily encounters, our tears and our laughter, and raise them to the level of an epic story: a tale with heroes and villains; beautiful places and dank dungeons; glorious battles resulting in tremendous victories fought against immeasurable odds and ignominious defeats causing our brethren to shake their heads in sorrow.

Several years ago I facilitated a conference panel. We panelists hoped to explore, through specific aspects of our own histories, events that shaped our movement lives, and our consciences as disabled activists. Three of us shared stories for about forty-five minutes with a couple hundred people.

When we finished, the most exciting part of the workshop began. We left half our time for audience participation. It was not enough. Everyone in the audience, it seemed, had a story they wished to share. One panelist kept whispering to me that we had to find a way to record all these stories. All of us glowed with an excitement so vibrant it seemed visible. Many people believed their stories demanded telling. The room thrilled to a feeling of community and oneness as we shared mutual struggles. We all broke through visible and invisible barriers to a newfound group freedom and appreciation.

This reaction reinforced my belief in our common identity. I began to concentrate more and more on our shared experiences, beliefs, desires, and feelings. Always possessed of a passion for the debate about language I began to accelerate that interest into a new passion: the concept of a disability culture and its potential meaning.

One of the most important aspects of disability culture, I perceived, was the concept of heroes. As I looked around at the people with whom I interacted I began to see and hear them in a new way. I began to think of many of my friends and colleagues as heroes.

I defined a hero simply as someone who did something courageous. Many of my acquaintances fit this definition. I knew people in every community performed heroic deeds; people who were well known and those who were anonymous. I knew, by the nature of the way people with disabilities in this society are treated, there had to be heroes with disabilities in every community. People who rose above everyday routine to act in some way beyond the expected and into the exceptional.

It was not a long leap from the notion of heroes to the concept of myth. People with disabilities have struggled to be liberated from an oppressive society. This kind of fight lends itself not only to heroes, but also to fascinating stories. This is not a nationalistic struggle, but a human one. It begged mythic telling.

When I began this adventure I knew little about scholarly definitions of mythology. But I knew the struggle of people with disabilities, our struggle, was an epic one. Despite my academic background as a historian this was not a story I wanted to tell in a straightforward manner. Myth is more accessible to the average listener than history. Myth permits us to be creative and expand our tales into stories that may be repeated and retold for generations. Myth can place our battles into a universal language understood by every culture.

I first read Joseph Campbell's *The Hero with a Thousand Faces* after deciding to proclaim our mythic lives. Campbell became known to many Americans when Bill Moyers conducted a series of interviews with him on Public Broadcasting Stations. Campbell argued the prime function of myth is to supply symbols that carry the human spirit forward. Each individual I'll discuss in the remainder of this essay has done exactly that. Each has moved us from some kind of static state to a more dynamic one.

My first hero is Helen Kutz, my mentor in this movement. I have laughed and cried with her. I have fought with her. I have celebrated with her. I have learned from her and I have taught her. Because she encouraged me to take talents I developed in a world where I knew little about disability, and use them to help both my people and myself, she will always remain the single person I identify more than anyone else as my hero.

When Helen arrived at the University of Oklahoma (OU) campus in the mid-1970s she had to schedule her classes at least one hour apart from each other. Why? If she needed a bathroom she had to have time to go home. No wheelchair accessible bathrooms existed on the University campus. When I required bathroom accessibility in the early 1980s this was no longer a concern. Helen, and others like her, changed the landscape of the University.

Going to the bathroom is no big deal—until we can't. Then it looms as one of life's biggest, and most, insistent problems. People needing this kind of accessibility today at OU probably never heard of the people who made their lives considerably simpler. But their actions impacted generations to come.

Campbell wrote, "The hero, therefore, is the man or woman who has been able to battle past his personal and local historical limitations…" I might append, the hero possesses a vision of changing the present to make the future a more comfortable place.

Another hero with a disability is a man few people outside of his hometown know. He is a quiet man, an unprepossessing man. In his calm way he became a hero.

When I worked as Executive Director at Norman's independent living center I saw Johnny almost daily. He'd show up at our office about the same time each day, bringing with him a few pieces of candy to offer our staff, and anyone else who happened to be around. He always had a smile on his face and a way of looking at whatever happened in his life as positive. He'd usually stay about fifteen minutes, chat with anyone who had a free moment or two, and then be on his way.

A year or so after first noticing Johnny's daily stops at our offices I realized he visited others as well. Like a mail carrier, he followed a route. We may have been the least important visit he made.

His path brought him most often to people who couldn't leave their homes, or who had fallen ill, or who needed a friend. Johnny realized these daily visitations filled people with joy. They became the most important actions he could take at that point in his life, both for himself and others.

The simple action of showing up in someone else's life on a routine basis became heroic because this man moved past his own limitations to soothe others. He did not preach, but his subtle support changed people's lives, and in many cases led those he visited to begin their own practice of visiting and comforting others. Campbell wrote that the hero brings wisdom back to humanity to renew his community. This man did exactly that and we all benefited from it.

My last example of heroism is Candace, a friend who is deaf from a brain injury. Today most people who know her consider deafness to be her primary disability. Few have heard her stories about how she had to write everything down after her injury so she would remember what she had to do and where she had to go. Or that when she went to college she took copious notes so as not to forget the content of the lectures she attended. Or that she worked all day and attended college at night.

These activities in and of themselves are imbued with heroism. But Candace did not perform these actions with greater glory in mind. She simply wanted to get by and make her way in a world that didn't care about her brain injury or her deafness.

Her journey is more remarkable because of her isolation. She did not know about a disability rights movement until long after she completed these tasks. She only knew what she had to do to make her dreams come true.

Campbell says that the hero's ultimate task is to communicate to people who insist on the exclusive evidence of their senses. When we hear comments like, "I'd rather be dead than disabled," we shudder at this contemptuous, naïve devaluing of our lives. But we also have some understanding of it. The comment is based on a feeling that to lose one of our senses, one of our primary functions, is so unthinkable that it is unbearable. We know this is false because we have all learned to live with our disabilities, and sometimes to revel in them, for the insights and experiences they bring. The heroes among us relay that revelation to others.

The stories of our heroes are underrated and too often untold. They comprise one part of the wealth of our experience.

We have much to bemoan. We also have much to celebrate. As a group, and as individuals, we, those of us with disabilities are living heroic lives. We need to recognize our feats and not be fearful of forging them into the epic stories they deserve.

Mythology is a universal language. It includes a set of symbols, such as heroes, placed in a context anyone can understand. Some myths are more complex than others. But all have the advantage of sharing traits common to all humans. As those of us with disabilities enter into the world of mythology we have an opportunity to take the excitement of our daily lives and translate it into stories that can be relayed to people of all languages, beliefs, and desires.

REFERENCES

Baldwin, James, *No Name in the Street* (New York: Doubleday, 1972).

Campbell, Joseph, *The Hero with a Thousand Faces* (Princeton: Princeton, 1949).

Zola, Irving Kenneth, *Missing Pieces: A Chronicle of Living with a Disability* (Philadelphia: Temple, 1983).

WE ARE WHO WE ARE...SO WHO ARE WE?

◆

Musings on the path to a definition of "Disability Culture."

[In the mid-1990s the idea of a culture of disability created controversy. Whenever we broached the topic we became embroiled in debates. Did such a culture exist? If it did, what constituted it? What did it mean? Would a disability culture be helpful or harmful for people with disabilities and the disability rights movement? This August 1996 *MAINSTREAM* essay served as a brief explanation about "disability culture." I hoped it would help frame the debate. I believe it did. The phrase "disability culture" has now become commonplace. Disability culture is perceived as an everyday part of our lives. I still use the one-paragraph definition provided at the conclusion of this piece so often I printed it on the back of my business card.]

Saturday morning. The sun shines. I sit contentedly in my living room chair fulfilling a volunteer commitment. Baking pleasantly in the warmth and the light, I am energized. I finish the volunteer work; I complete some light reading; I retrieve my pile of disability culture research notecards waiting to be organized and filed. I feel productive. I am contemplative. Before I can stop myself my brain races into an approach and definition of disability culture I think might be livable.

How many cultural definitions or characteristics might one find in the above paragraph? Sun-worshipper? Volunteer? Workaholic? Reader? Philosopher?

What would make any of the above words into cultures? What would make me a member of such a culture?

It's been ten years since I first started mulling over the concept of disability culture. During the first five of those years I was a passionate, though sporadic, investigator of the concept. I facilitated and participated in some panels that discussed the subject. I began to promote the concept.

During the past five years I have moved from passionate explorer to "acknowledged authority" (and to what cultures does *that* appellation belong?). I am writer, promoter, advocate, expert, co-founder of the second institution specifically about disability culture, teacher, student, poet, and so forth.

Yet when someone asks me for a definition of disability culture I am hard-pressed to respond in a way that will make sense to both of us. I have never had a handy one sentence or paragraph explanation of the concept.

One reason for this is that the words themselves are full of controversy. "Disability" is defined differently in various parts of the world, by distinct cultures, by diverse outlooks on life. What once was a disability may no longer be. For example, certain visual needs can be corrected with the use of glasses (and who hears the phrase spectacle-bound?).

The United Nations has spent more than ten years and who knows how many people hours attempting to define disability, handicap, and impairment for a classification system. The endeavor continues.

"Culture" is a word just as value-laden. There may be as many definitions as there are people working in the field of "cultural studies" (which did not exist several years ago). I am loosely defining that field, for the purpose of this essay, as anyone who chooses to pursue cultural issues.

When I began to write about disability culture I felt much more comfortable with my ability to define "disability" than "culture." So I started searching for definitions of culture. I quickly learned how many definitions and controversies about the word and its meanings existed. I looked it up in the dictionary.

The 1973 Random House Unabridged Dictionary, which happens to be the one I use at work, defines culture as "the sum total of ways of living built up by a group of human beings and transmitted from one generation to another."

Shortly after copying this definition I came across another. I don't know its origin, but its definition is a "totality of socially transmitted behavior patterns, arts, beliefs, institutions, and all other products of human work and thought characteristic of a community or population."

I did find one other definition useful: one is a part of a culture if they think they are. I did not note the source of this definition—it seemed too simple, I guess. But the phrase, or a variation of it, shows up frequently, including in my own writing.

The problem with these definitions is the same obstacle that is the problem with any definition that is not commonly accepted—they generate controversy.

So, as I sat radiating in the sun this morning, I started thinking about the definition and my inability to develop a definition of disability culture that gave me comfort.

I seemed to have hit upon some clues. Let's see...

What, I wondered for the first time, if I analyzed similarities that the various definitions of culture seemed to share? An appallingly simple answer resulted: Each definition of culture is trying to place the concept in some sort of context. Either one is a part of a culture because one fits the context or one is not for the same reason.

What then is the reason for such emphatic need to develop context and ensure its integrity? Henry Adams wrote more than a century ago, "order is the dream of man, chaos is the law of the universe." Context is order. If we can figure out to which culture, or context, we belong, then we can put the rest of humanity in order, that is in context, either as a member or an outcast of our culture, our context.

As any activist in any social, political, cultural, or other movement can verify, belonging is about naming, claiming, and proclaiming. We all do this all the time. I claim, for example, to have a disability, to be a writer, to be a husband, and to be a father. Naming these identities is the same as claiming them.

When I say I'm a writer I also proclaim myself a member of a group of people who write. Others may write who do not make such a proclamation. Are they not writers? Indeed, they are. But they choose not to claim to be a member of the group.

Meaning they refuse, for whatever reason, to put themselves into the context, the cohort of the group of writers.

If I find out you are a writer who does not choose to proclaim yourself by that label I can either choose to accept you as you are or try to change you. In either case I am making a choice to put you into an order, a context. Who am I to do this to you?

Exactly.

The debate about definitions is not a debate primarily about the literal meaning of a word. It's a debate about power.

Who has the power to create and apply definitions? In this specific case, who has the power to create and apply definitions of culture? For the most part, the people who have claimed—and proclaim—that power have been academicians in the fields of anthropology, psychology, history, sociology, and other so-called social sciences.

There may be all sorts of reasons for this act of power. People who are formulating definitions may believe they have the most knowledge about these concepts and therefore the most right to implement their own beliefs. They may just as easily believe they have spent many years of their lives acquiring this knowledge and because of it the position to formulate definitions. They may also believe that others who have not experienced their long quest for knowledge and position have little right to question their judgment. Or they could just as easily fear that when someone questions their judgment they will lose their power.

In any case, the motivation for claiming expertise is power. The power to name, the power to define, the power to proclaim, the power to place people into a context, an order which fits the vision of the person doing the naming, claiming, and proclaiming.

Many people who have had the power to define culture have chosen to state, in one variation or another that you cannot be a part of a culture because you think you are. Why not? Who makes this rule?

If I choose to say I am a member of the disability culture who is anyone else to oppose this proclamation? A doctor, social worker, psychologist, politician, (and so forth) who say I do not have a disability? Who are they to make this judgment? Do I have a disability if I think I do? Who is the expert, the person in power, who can argue I do not have this right?

If I do not give them the power no one has these rights. If I do give them the power, then everyone has these rights.

This makes the debate, the controversy over definition, a fight over who has the power of naming, claiming, and proclaiming a disability culture. I believe I have this right for myself. I am unwilling to give it to anyone else. I have the power.

Of course, the entire preceding debate is moot. Because while we may argue about its existence, or characteristics, the culture itself goes on with or without us.

Art is burgeoning. Writing is increasing. Teaching is taking place. Children are learning about their history. Values are being explored. Music is being composed. Humor is generating laughter. Members of the culture are being born and dying. Life goes on.

The debate itself, while perhaps irrelevant, goes on as well. And because I am part of that debate, I offer a definition of disability culture as follows:

> People with disabilities have forged a group identity. We share a common history of oppression and a common bond of resilience. We generate art, music, literature, and other expressions of our lives and our culture, infused from our

experience of disability. Most importantly, we are proud of ourselves as people with disabilities. We claim our disabilities with pride as part of our identity. We are who we are: we are people with disabilities.

You now have the choice to accept, reject, or refine this definition. The power is yours—if you take it.

DIS-ING DEFINITIONS:
AN EPIPHANY ABOUT THE
MYTHS OF (DIS)ABILITIES

[*MAINSTREAM* published this essay exactly one year following the preceding one. It's another attempt to explore language in a way that might move forward discussions of what we, as a disability rights movement, think we wish to attain.]

Language can be a bane of human rights movements. What do we call ourselves? What do others call us? Do labels intersect with models of freedom? Can descriptions of who we are liberate us from yokes of oppression? Do we automatically imprison ourselves as soon as we turn to classifications?

For many years I have been writing, talking, and thinking about language. Like my colleagues across the world in the disability rights movement I have described myself as an individual with a disability, using the preferred term "disability" for myriad conditions in combination with "people first" language where the condition of "disability" is an adjective describing one aspect of a person.

Lately, I have become quite dissatisfied with this description of myself, my peers, and those outside of these conditions, whom I've labeled "nondisabled." Troubling doubts insinuate themselves into my heretofore solid foundation of where I fit into a disability rights movement.

I am not alone.

In almost every audience there is someone who says something like, "we all have disabilities." My response to this statement has been that, like most generalizations, it is so broad it is meaningless. When one is immersed in a political struggle to establish certain rights as fundamental to existence, then a group must clearly identify itself as "other" or "outsider" from the dominant mainstream, or "insider," group. Those who fill (maybe even overflow) social margins can then be rendered less "outsiders" by attaining concrete achievements. New laws, better educational outcomes, higher employment levels, or (since this is about disabilities) curb cuts or interpreter services, enable them to acquire "insider" status.

All of a sudden, though not sudden at all, every aspect of the above paragraph gives me a "paradigmache." Is "insider" status truly the goal?

Looking at language and "insider" status, I propose to enlist a commonly used dictionary to provide typical definitions about disability.[1] Using the following words and noting how they are portrayed may lead us (or at least me) to a new way of looking at the issue, condition, status, and way of life called "disability:"

Disabled: "incapacitated by illness, injury, or wounds; broadly: physically or mentally impaired."

Impaired: "being in a less than perfect or whole condition: as a: handicapped or functionally defective…"

Handicapped: "having a physical or mental disability that substantially limits activity, esp. in relation to employment or education"

Defective: "imperfect in form or function"

Sickness: "ill health"

Health: "the condition of being sound in body, mind, and spirit; esp.: freedom from physical disease or pain"

Illness: "an unhealthy condition of body or mind"

Freedom: "the absence of necessity, coercion, or constraint in choice or action"

Oppression: "an unjust or cruel exercise of authority or power"

Cure: "to restore to health, soundness, or normality"

Normality: Undefined

Using the preceding definitions, everyone does indeed have a disability if it is defined as "impairment," that is, being less than perfect. Until recently, I would simply have thought that is too broad an interpretation to be useful and dismissed it. But what if I embrace the concept of universal disability rather than sweeping it away?

---

1.   Definitions taken from Merriam-Webster's Collegiate Dictionary: Tenth Edition (Springfield, MA: Merriam-Webster Inc., 1996).

The most immediate result is that a (possibly) artificial distinction between two groups of people—"disabled" and "nondisabled" is eliminated. This obliteration also wipes out several continuums of "insider/outsider" statuses. Depending on one's point of view and identification, "insider" and "outsider" roles may change meanings from one person to the next and even in the same person over time. But "insider/outsider" roles about disability can only continue to be developed as long as we perceive certain individuals to have disabilities.

When we persist in these "outsider/insider" identifications we don't merely play into the definitions of our oppressors, we thrust ourselves into those definitions so eagerly that we, as much as our oppressors, perpetuate the myths of (dis)abilities. We fall into a seductive trap of utilizing the dominant paradigms to control the way we think about ourselves.

I believe that each of us involved in a rights movement has the same goal: to be treated as equally as the most privileged member of society. We easily obtain proof that equality does not exist, the most obvious demonstrations generally being lack of education, employment, and political status. We are also treated differently before the law. In United States history, people who have not: owned property, been white men, been physically able to get into a voting booth, or been able to read the language of a ballot, among other groups, have all been legally disfranchised.

Knowing that we are being treated differently before the law, we work to attain a kind of equilibrium between those who are and who are not privileged. We accomplish this by changing the law so that people who do not own property, are not white men, are unable to get into a voting booth, or read a ballot, among other groups, all become legally enfranchised. We work to change the social structure so that education, employment, and political statuses become reformed in such a way that our group becomes a part of the privileged.

While we strive to become "insiders," part of the social mainstream, or the "privileged," we, like many have-nots, are snared in a web of hegemony, wanting and working to become in some way like our oppressors—dominant over (or more privileged than) some other group—so that we see and feel and partake in a concrete shift moving from "outsider" to "insider" status. In the struggle, we sometimes forget that the original goal of all rights movements, to be treated equally with the most privileged members of society, should also be applied to everyone, not only our particular group.

There are those reading these words who will have a problem with the use of the terms "oppression and oppressors." But, according to the dictionary definition, those who unjustly use authority and power are oppressors. When difference is used, as it routinely has been, to transform groups of people into "outsiders" and then submerge and suppress these groups educationally, economically, socially, and politically, then "insiders" have indeed become oppressors.

"Outsiders" become people who escape fitting neatly into mainstream definitions of normality—which according to the same dictionary, don't exist! This circuitous path of analyzing definitions of disability leads to the (il)logical(?) conclusion that no one is "normal," therefore everyone is! The logic becomes convoluted because the definitions both depend, and turn, on themselves. We are unable to be clear about these words and concepts because they are so extremely artificial, that is, made up.

This, too, is not earth-shattering. We all make up ways to describe ourselves, that's what language is, a way to communicate. But who makes the language? "Insiders." Those of us who fall away from whatever happens to be a typical definition of "normality," become "outsiders." It does not matter that "normality" is undefined, because "insiders" believe themselves to possess the knowledge of what it is. Undefined, it is much easier to maintain "insider" status by changing it when it is convenient.

To use the example of voting once more, "insiders" have changed throughout the course of United States history from white, male property-owners to non-property owners, women, and many more people. But enfranchisement is not completely inclusive. Many groups remain disenfranchised, perhaps the most obvious being those individuals under a certain chronological age. But those of us who do vote have frequently changed from "outsider" to "insider." As "insider" status regarding voting has changed, so has the concept of "normality" in the polling booth.

This web of intricate patterns, circles, and snares is a trap because the people controlling the web are "insiders" and, short of revolution, only they have the power to change it. What power, then, do we, as "outsiders" possess?

We hold the power to change the environment, to not be caught in the web, to not be seduced by becoming "insiders" ourselves. We have the power to change our own pursuit of freedom to become equal with, not with our oppressors, but everyone. I have an old button with the slogan, "*No one is free when others are oppressed.*" If I, or my group, become so successful in our rights quest that we become "insiders," then someone else remains oppressed. In this scenario, we also unfortunately become part of the system, most frequently by joining its workforce (known in the 1960s as being co-opted) or becoming so attached to the material possessions and security of the mainstream that we struggle to be a part of its flow, no matter how disinclined we may believe we are to actually fit into the status quo.

This is not what I want as my life path. How can I change my life, my work, my struggle, so that I no longer perceive becoming an "insider" as the ultimate goal?

The myths of (dis)abilities (and other "outsider" groups) are perpetuated because of a willingness by both "outsider" and "insider" groups to assimilate the standard definitions of terms and their concomitant oppressive results. Shatter the definitions, alter the myths, destroy the "outsider"/"insider" dichotomy and what remains?

Few of us know, because we ("outsiders" and "insiders," ironically, together) have been so successfully seduced into the mainstream that we linger, and even wallow, in the paradigms of our oppressors. The current worldview that defines the concept of "disability" fits into the "insider/outsider" paradigms.

Reaching these conclusions have been most difficult, but now comes the truly hard part: I know that I am no longer willing to be categorized as an "outsider" because I am no longer interested in becoming an "insider."

What do I become? That remains to be seen. I don't have an answer.

Until recently, I also did not have the question. Until setting these thoughts down, the answer was unknowable because the query was unthinkable.

Future thoughts and writings must incorporate responses to these newly-established opportunities. I look forward to the possibilities.

DEVIANTS, INVALIDS, AND ANTHROPOLOGISTS[1]: CROSS-CULTURAL PERSPECTIVES ON CONDITIONS OF DISABILITY IN ONE ACADEMIC DISCIPLINE: A REVIEW OF *DISABILITY AND CULTURE.*

◆

Eds. Benedicte Ingstad and Susan Reynolds Whyte (Berkeley: University of California Press, 1995) [pp. 307]

[During the 1990s I published articles in disability magazines and academic journals about disability. In this piece I responded to a request from the editor of *Disability and Rehabilitation* to author a book review. I attempted a critical exploration in this May 1996 review of a book, which I found both frustrating and provocative.]

---

1. A play on the title of Chapter One, "Deviants, Invalids, and Freedom Fighters: Historical Perceptions of People with Disabilities in the United States," in my 1994 monograph *Investigating a Culture of Disability: Final Report.*

This is a critical, expansive review that may be somewhat unfair to the editors and authors of an important book. Turnabout, some say, is fair play. People with disabilities have been fair game for academics, helping professionals, politicians, and anyone else who has sought a hand in our affairs for centuries. Generalizations, ideas about what is best for us, and who knows what's best about us, have been essentially unquestioned for millennia. Similar attitudes prevail throughout this anthology, within a quest for answers to difficult questions, a desire to comprehend diverse cultures, and an amazing array of definitions of disability itself.

Buried on page 247 in one of the two editors' many essays is the statement that recent anthropological writings stress the importance of giving an account of the researcher's background. Appropriate and fair enough. I am a historian by academic training, an activist by experience, and have recently begun to consider myself a philosopher by choice. I am a middle-class, middle-aged, white male of Jewish ancestry who has a disability. Much of my identity is entwined with my perception of myself as an individual with a disability and my self-identified life mission to promote pride in the history, activities, and cultural identity of individuals with disabilities throughout the world.

Benedicte Ingstad, the editor referred to in the preceding paragraph, is the mother of a son with a disability. She conveys this information on the same page she stresses the importance of identifying the researcher's background. In addition to the biographical paragraph about her in the back of the book, this is the third, and final, essay in which she claims authorship. It is the next-to-last entry in the book. It is not until this point she shares this very important component of her background.

What does this have to do with the rest of the book? There are fourteen essays by twelve authors. There are apparently six male authors, one of whom is a member of an ethnic minority and has a disability, which is alluded to during the course of his essay. The remainder of the authors seem to be of European or North American origin. The editors choose to use the terms "Northern" and "Southern" to describe Western and non-Westernized cultures. Aside from the startling omission of Australia and New Zealand from Westernized status (they describe "Northern" as Europe and North America), there is a more serious question concerning the ability of the researchers to understand "Southern" cultures when only one author appears to be from such a culture himself.

This concern stems not from pre-conceived notions of any particular researcher's capabilities, but from warnings contained in the book itself. For example, from the Introduction: "But we want to be wary of a pitfall of cultural juxtaposition: our tendency to look at other cultures in terms of our own problems and thus to fail to grasp the premises upon which other people are operating."

A warning well taken. Why, then, are there not more contributions from representatives of these "Southern" countries? Value-laden statements send shock waves from some of the essays. Again from the Introduction: "Although a bodily or mental deficit does indeed function as a lack for which one is entitled to receive something, the giver may also be recompensed in achieving virtue." Buried in an endnote on page 26 is the idea that someone with a disability is owed something for a condition that is unequivocally considered negative and the idea that goodness is a reward for this offering. This concise statement is a description of the charity mentality of aiding helpless cripples that people with disabilities are now rebelling against all over the world. In another essay, Ingstad states: "People with mental retardation necessarily have to be represented by their parents, or close kin…" This statement would be disputed by members of People First and by many community members who work with individuals with mental retardation. How much of this statement is influenced by Ingstad's role as a parent of a son with a disability (she does not state what disability) and how much by her background as a Norwegian, where family may be more important than community, unlike other parts of the world?

There are two reasons for devoting so much energy to these statements. First, the editors contribute five of the fourteen essays, slightly more than one-third, and have had a hand in encouraging the development of a majority of the remainder, influencing the development and execution of this anthology more significantly than usual. Second, as these examples are intended to demonstrate, the emphasis on cross-cultural sensitivity is easier to admonish than to administer.

Facts about the books itself: The fourteen essays include an Introduction and an Epilogue. The remaining twelve contributions are divided into two sections—"Disability, Cosmology, and Personhood," and "Social Contexts of Disability." Nations included in these articles are Belgium, Botswana, Germany, Kenya, Malaysia, New Zealand, Nicaragua, Norway, Somalia, Sweden, Tanzania, Turkey, Uganda, United Kingdom, United States, and Zaire.

Both the "Introduction" and the "Epilogue" comprise interesting, stand-alone chapters that provide an appropriate beginning and a provocative conclusion. Each section is introduced with a short prologue that seems obtrusive and unnecessary. Articles contain bibliographies and endnotes. In many of the articles, the endnotes are full of minutiae, interrupting the flow of the story.

The variety of definitions about disability begins on the first page of the Introduction, "A preliminary common-sense definition of disability might be that it is a lack or limitation of competence. We usually think of disability in contrast to an ideal of normal capacity to perform particular activities and to play one's role in social life." Even with continuous redefining of disability there is a sense that there is a "Northern" view of disabling conditions, which is accepted by all. There is little exploration about the contentiousness of perceptions of disability exemplified in all aspects of American life, including organizations of and for people with disabilities. This may be attributable to the idealized status accorded the late Robert Murphy, author of a classic analysis of living with a disability in the United States, *The Body Silent*. One chapter is excerpted from this work.

Murphy's status as an anthropologist and a person living with an acquired disability combined to make him an authority about disabling conditions. Unfortunately, he tends to be presented as *the* authority. Even when writing in the 1980s, there were also others writing about life with a disability from other perspectives. For the most part, these other authors were hidden in non-traditional publications and have not yet dented the mainstream, academic market. A distinct lack of knowledge about other colorful and scholarly authors such as Carol Gill, Harlan Hahn, Paul Longmore, Adolf Ratzka, and the majority of the work of Irving Kenneth Zola is missing from the entire book. More disturbing is the assumption that what Murphy had to say in the late 1980s would stand unchanged in the mid-1990s. Murphy's own description of the liminal status of disability might just as aptly apply to his own work—standing at the crossroads between perceptions of disability as a negative condition making it difficult to function in society and today's refined idea of disability as a natural process of life which is not only *not* completely negative, but has characteristics non-disabled society could benefit from emulating.

The book provides extensive ideas about defining disability in various ways in "Southern" countries, despite its monolithic portrayal in the "North." In vivid contrast, the term, "culture" is never discussed.

Although all contributions are made by anthropologists who evidently intend to speak primarily to each other, it is astonishing that there is no awareness of the vigorous, ongoing debate over the use and concepts of "culture." In my own work, people seldom question how disability is defined, but are continually challenging how "culture" is employed. The conclusion I come to is that both concepts need to be explored individually and together in rigorous discussion.

Patrick Devlieger succinctly explores key questions raised throughout the book in "Why Disabled? The Cultural Understanding of Physical Disability in an African Society:"

> Looking at disability from a cultural point of view starts with asking questions such as, What does disability mean in a certain society? How is the status of the person with a disability determined by the culture in which he/she lives? What are the most important issues when talking about disability in a certain society?"

The concept of rehabilitation itself, which is also painted as a unified concept without much shading, is one such issue. Despite the sensitivity and awareness demonstrated throughout the book that "Southern" cultures differ significantly from "Northern" ones, there is almost no question that rehabilitation or Community-based Rehabilitation (CBR) should be exported to these countries:

> If CBR can be perceived not as something *new* [author's emphasis] that mainly needs expertise from outside but as a way of mobilizing the community itself, it stands a much better chance of being sustained. This is the way the model is intended to be used, but because insufficient effort is usually put into examining these local communities *before* [author's emphasis] a program is started, it does not always turn out this way.

Within the United States especially there is currently a national debate over the efficacy of rehabilitation programs. People with disabilities who mobilized in an impressive fashion to advocate for the passage of the Americans with Disabilities Act are unable to form any kind of stable coalitions over this issue. While being sensitive to issues of other cultures perhaps we need to retrench and resensitize ourselves to our own culture prior to uncritical export of "Northern" institutions into "Southern" colonies.

Throughout the book is a theme of respecting cultural diversity and difference. Yet, in the final chapter, Susan Reynolds Whyte states, "rehabilitation emphasizes integration into a society of similar people through individual effort and social compensation, and the unspoken agreement to identify difference and pretend it does not exist..." As people within the "Northern" countries are becoming proud of our identity as individuals with disabilities and members of a disability community, perhaps that is a primary cause of rebellion against the rehabilitation system. It may also be a reason not to export rehabilitation to cultures whose diversity we claim to respect, and who, as frequently exhibited in this book, are already proud of who they are the way they are. Adapting the "Northern" way of rehabilitation may be of more benefit to the givers than to recipients.

Some essays include historical perspectives. But few authors delve earlier than the phase of individuals with disabilities leaving some sort of institutionalized setting to moving into a seemingly integrated environment. There are frequent comparisons of "Northern" institutional rehabilitation entities with "Southern" pre-institutional rehabilitation life. Many authors contend that analyzing the more positive aspects of, for example, "Southern" family and community life could be beneficial to "Northern" countries. While we are exploring cultural diversity, we may want to explore our own diverse, cultural pasts and look at what life may have been like in pre-institutional days. We may have more to learn from the diversity of our own history than we can imagine.

Disability and Culture is a fascinating book, both for what is and what is not within its covers. The editors have accomplished a provocative study. Criticisms of it need to be tempered with the knowledge that it is one of the best compilations so far developed. Both interesting and provocative, it could serve as a textbook or an addition to a community library. The many gaps it contains shows more than anything else how much further we have to go to create a sturdy foundation of scholarly work in disability studies and to recognize the work already in existence that is difficult to access.

Final words come from Whyte's Epilogue, "Disability between Discourse and Experience," and reflect the content both of the book and of this review:

> Do people with impairments accept the constructions of themselves that are offered? If they adopt the discourse, how do they transform it? Or do they resist it? In what contexts do they accept, ignore, contest, or rework a given discourse?

"OH, DON'T YOU ENVY US OUR PRIVILEGED LIVES?" A REVIEW OF THE DISABILITY CULTURE MOVEMENT

[Ten years after voicing my first tentative ideas about disability culture I offered a bibliographic summation of the developing movement in the August 1997 *Disability and Rehabilitation*.]

The fishing is free with your disability
You don't need a licence like the rest.
Movies are half the price, well isn't that nice?
And the parking spots are nothing but the best.

Well, don't you wish that you were disabled?
Disabled is the better way to be.
With crutches, canes and braces, wheelchairs to run races
Don't you wish that you were just like me?

The deaf have got sign language,
the blind have got their dogs
Their loyal trusted guides are at their sides.
Well everyone has their vices, but we've got our devices
Oh, don't you envy us our privileged lives?[1]

INCUBATION

Thirty people met in October 1996, surrounded by the grandeur of Santa Fe, New Mexico, to discuss the concept of disability culture. One comment in particular, from these two intense days, begs preliminary consideration in a review about disability culture.

The individual who made the statement is a woman of color who observed that white people with disabilities might need to create a culture out of disabling conditions because we are so lacking in other cultural identifications. Several of us remarked that we knew a number of women of color who also have disabilities who consider their primary culture to be that of disability. The woman simply could not fathom these women were being completely truthful about themselves.

As I continue to mull this commentary about white people with disabilities I believe it has some merit. Some, but not complete, validity. As I have wrestled with the question of identity for most of my life, I do believe that my background as white has been somewhat limiting in my cultural identification. Somewhat, but not totally, confining.

In my brief interactions with my colleague from this meeting I surmised that her identity emerged not only from her being a person of color, but also being a resident of a large Eastern city with a large population of people of color, and continuing to live in a similar urban situation. As those of us from the middle and western parts of the U.S. will attest, there is often a vast difference in style, if not more fundamental aspects of our lives, from one area of the country to another, including but not encompassing the changes one experiences going from larger metropolises to smaller cities to rural areas.

The woman who prompted these reflections is also someone who works in an academic environment, which in and of itself has engendered so many descriptions of difference it would be overkill to add to them here. But to throw in some irony, this woman's academic situation is unusual. She works at an institution geared toward people with disabilities different from her own.

I have no desire to attempt an amateur analysis of this woman. But I think her resistance to the concept of a disability culture is instructive. Most fundamentally, there seems to be an almost inevitable gut response to first hearing of the notion of disability culture—either in favor of or opposition to the idea. But the intense, emotional response itself is a sign that the concept is a powerful one.

I suppose this should not be a surprise. Culture and disability are both value- and identity-laden core beliefs. When they are discussed and challenged people respond with a vehemence, which values and identity demand.

Second, no one is a product of just one culture, although many of us choose to identify with—or despite no initiative of our own are identified with—a primary culture. It may be religious, ethnic, skin color, occupation, geographic location, or many other possibilities. I know of no proponent of disability culture who argues that we belong to only one cultural group.

Third, because disability and culture are such value-and identity-laden terms, which at least potentially impact us all, any discussion about them becomes open to everyone. Embodied in these discussions are our hopes and fears, our dreams and nightmares, our realities and illusions.

I begin this article with the preceding discussion because as academic as we might wish to make and dissect the concept of disability culture, it remains an extremely personal vision. Because of this inescapable fact and because of my own training in the academic discipline of history I always try to incorporate as clearly as possible my own biases and shortcomings:

1) When discussing disability culture I focus on cross-disability culture, meaning a movement that crosses all disabilities and all cultural groups. I do not do this because I believe the meaning of disability culture is the same for everyone, but because I (and the discussion) have to start somewhere;

2) I write about disability culture primarily in the United States, because, once again, one has to start somewhere. There is a thriving, energetic, intellectual discussion of disability culture in England. One of these days I hope to experience it firsthand and write about it. The concept of disability culture has also excited people of every nationality that has encountered and discussed it;

3) I examine primarily a British—influenced middle class history and culture. The reason for this is endemic to American history. This background has permeated our national history, politics, culture, and most importantly, the people who have recorded it. It is in part a reaction to this characteristic of our academic settings that disciplines such as social and cultural history, ethnic studies, and women's studies developed. It is also one of the primary motivations for the development of disability studies. Discussions of disability culture from a non-British-based, non-middle class perspective are as needed as they are for other topics;

4) I have always been a fan of both high- and low-brow culture. I am also an advocate of blending academic research and knowledge with non-academic research and knowledge and endeavor to write from that slant;

5) I am a white, middle class male and am writing from that perspective, and, finally,

6) I have discussed my reflections about debates over the terms "disability" and "culture" in detail elsewhere and will not repeat them here.[2]

INFANCY

Well, don't you wish that you were disabled?
Disabled is the better way to be.
When we go out it's really neat,
we're always sure we'll get a seat
Oh, don't you wish that you were just like me?

In the mid-1980s sporadic discussions about the existence of a culture of disability surfaced. The first two documented publications about disability culture appeared in the *Proceedings* that followed the 1984 Conference of the Association on Handicapped Student Service Programs in Post-Secondary Education (then AHSSPPE, now AHEAD, Association of Higher Education and Disability).

David Pfeiffer, then of Suffolk University and Andrea Schein, then of the University of Massachusetts—Boston, each presented papers entitled "Is There a Culture of Disability?" Both scholars traced the roots of the meaning of "culture" to anthropological origins. Schein contended that "culture" has taken on various meanings over the past hundred years, including an appreciation of the finer things in life, a distinctive body of customs, and a learned body of traditions within a society. She then linked this evolution of terminology to an evolution of thinking about disability.

> The issue of disability has passed through a mirror from being perceived as an unfortunate medical problem to a new recognition of the denial of basic citizenship rights to a disenfranchised minority group.

Schein concluded, "All over the United States, there are people with a wide range of disabilities who understand and share the central concepts of the disability sub-culture."

Pfeiffer argued that the culture of disability is learned.

In conclusion, when the artifacts, the mental products, the social organizations, and the coping mechanisms of disabled persons are brought together, it is seen that the culture is learned, shared, interrelated, cumulative, and diverse. A culture of disability does exist.[3]

The *Disability Rag & Resource* (formerly the *Disability Rag* and now revived as *The Ragged Edge*), *MAINSTREAM, Mouth, New Mobility, Accent On Living*, and other representatives of what might be labeled the "disability press"[4] have historically been the primary vehicles for exploration of this topic.

But despite the dubious statistics about our numbers, there are many among us who *do* understand, who are of common purpose: they are the Disabled Community…If we don't vigorously acknowledge disability to ourselves, and forge the Disabled Community, we will never be acknowledged.[5]

The most consistent, passionate, and persistent voice initially promoting the concept of disability culture has been that of psychologist Carol Gill:

If we neglect the cultural aspects of our movement, we will fail. There's only so far you can get with intellectual ideas, or even political clout. If you don't have your people fed and charged up, liking who they are and liking each other, wanting to stand by each other, you will fail.[6]

CHILDHOOD

The Disability Culture Movement began to assert itself, like a child exploring their world, in the early 1990s. Five notable actions occurred within three years of each other. First, Cheryl Marie Wade of Berkeley, California, one of the most recognized disability culture poets and performance artists in the United States, delivered a thundering welcome to our culture in an address to an organization devoted to the promotion of disability art and artists with disabilities. Her presentation began:

Disability culture. SAY WHAT? Aren't disabled people just isolated victims of nature or circumstance? Yes and no. True, we are far too often isolated. Locked away in the pits, closets, and institutions of enlightened societies everywhere. But there is a growing consciousness among us: 'THAT is not acceptable.' Because there is always an underground. Notes get passed among survivors. And the notes we're passing these days say, 'there's power in difference. Power. Pass the word.' Culture. It's about passing the word. And disability culture is passing the word that there's a new definition of disability and it includes power. Culture. New definitions, new inflections.[7]

Two events occurred in 1992. First, David Hevey of London authored *The Creatures Time Forgot: Photography and Disability Imagery*. No one had approached disability, disability art, and disability rights in a like manner. In the book's first chapter he states that he has, "attempted to register photographically the energy in the fightback of individual disabled people and the disability movement." As a photographer, Hevey is intensely conscious of how people observe the world and how the world observes back: "How the observed begin their own observing is a crucial question in all radical cultural practice and its relevance is critical for new disability photographic practices." He contends arbiters of social mores cannot be permitted to maintain a stranglehold on images of disability. Disabled people can utilize photography to analyze how they are portrayed and generally oppressed.

Hevey concludes, "oppressed people's culture is always undervalued and misrepresented by the dominant culture." Radical disability imagery must admit the panorama of experience, life, and action. The permanent route out of oppressive imagery begins with dismantling by caricature. An empowering, truly positive disability imagery must contain signs of pain, of reclamation of the body, marks of struggle and overcoming, and signs for a future.[8]

The second landmark of 1992 was also the first of two concrete manifestations of disability culture in the United States: the establishment of the Disabled Student Cultural Center at the University of Minnesota. This resulted from a research project among a student group studying disability issues that discerned the necessity for such an organization, then successfully convinced the University to seek funds to sponsor it. (G. Chelberg, personal communication, April 1992). The program has been an enormously successful one which not only continues to exist, but has branched out into other endeavors, most notably an annual Leadership Conference targeted to students with disabilities.

The second concrete manifestation was two-pronged: a 1993—94 U. S. Department of Education Research Fellowship I received to conduct research about disability culture, the first funding of its type, which culminated in a 250 page document, *Investigating a Culture of Disability: Final Report;*[9] and the 1994 founding of the not-for-profit Institute on Disability Culture, by my wife and partner, Lillian Gonzales Brown and myself, whose purpose is "promoting pride in the history, activities and cultural identity of individuals with disabilities throughout the world."

Coming full circle, in the finale of these five notable events, the National Endowment for the Arts recognized Cheryl Marie Wade's artistic contributions with an Arts Solo Theatre Artist's Fellowship in 1994, the first award of its kind to someone promoting disability culture.

ADOLESCENCE

> No one knows just what to call us which label should befall us,
> And they're some dandy terms from which to choose.
> My favourite's "wheel-chair bound" cause it has a bondage sound.
> Oh it's fun to guess what term they're going to use.
>
> Well, don't you wish that you were disabled?
> Disabled is the better way to be.
> There are special entrances in stores, they let us in
> through the back doors
> Oh, don't you wish that you were just like me?

Modern teenagers lead complicated and confused lives striving to assess their own life values and goals. Such is also true of the topic of disability culture. A bewildering array of sources, either devoted to or tangentially addressing this subject is in existence and growing every day. One of the most difficult aspects of researching disability culture has been the propensity for it to show up in nontraditional areas, such as organizational newsletters, or music, art, or writing that is not distributed in conventional ways. This has become even truer with the advent of the Internet and the multiplication of World Wide Web sites literally addressing millions of different people and topics.

When Investigating a Culture of Disability was published in 1994 I wrote that it had the most extensive bibliography to date about disability culture. It included a total of more than 250 citations, including: 65 books; 24 anthology articles; 99 magazine and journal articles; 20 newspaper and newsletter articles; 11 unpublished manuscripts; 50 films; 5 musical entries; and 8 cultural artifacts, including comics, calendars, and a poster. Yet, this too, was only a selected bibliography, highlighting the most important of 929 citations, entered in my own unpublished bibliography, into twenty-four computer database categories. As I write, the bibliographical count is 1181.[10]

Still, much is missing, including volumes of magazines and journals I have yet to locate, books I have to read, music to hear, videos to watch, resources that have escaped my attention, and, I am certain, a plethora of international commentaries unknown to me.[11]

So, as I contemplated ways to integrate vast bibliographic building blocks into my previous remarks about the evolution of the concept of disability culture, I decided to discuss a combination of the lesser—known and most important entries from each of three broad topic areas—Art, History, and Identity—to scratch the surface of disability culture. One caveat must be included here as well. Several years ago, I decided that I would not include items in my bibliography that I had not yet had a chance to read or review. The reason for this is that, until quite recently, too many people writing and furnishing critiques about disability products have done so from the older perspectives of viewing disability as a condition to be fixed or cured, rather than accepted and perceived as a natural process of living. I don't wish to promote these outmoded viewpoints in my own work. I choose, instead, to emphasize a "disability pride and culture model" of disability, which recognizes disability as a natural aspect of living.

ART

I have integrated the words of Jane Field's song, "The Fishing is Free," throughout this discussion because many people are able to accept the idea of a disability culture much more easily if they are able to feel it. There are so many examples of living with a disability infused into art that it is most difficult to choose a sampling. In a way this is good news. The culture is alive and well.

In alphabetical and categorical order, I begin with cartoonist John Callahan. He is noted for wickedly satiric depictions of all kinds of subjects. He is also a quadriplegic and recovering alcoholic who describes his life in an excellent autobiography, *Don't Worry, He Won't Get Far on Foot: The Autobiography of a Dangerous Man* (New York: Vintage, 1989). The title is taken from his cartoon of a posse coming upon an empty wheelchair in the desert and making the salient observation.[12]

An unusual, if not unique, figure in both art and disability was the Mexican painter Frida Kahlo. Her pictures, including many self-portraits, are devoted to themes of disability and pain. Kahlo's life is portrayed and much of her art included in Hayden Herrera's *Frida Kahlo: The Paintings* (New York: Harper Collins, 1991).

David Hevey's analytical abilities in *The Creatures Time Forgot: Photography and Disability Imagery* are not the only highlight of his book. He is also adept at his art of photography and showing why certain pictures and photographic exhibitions and campaigns do or do not reflect a modern consciousness about disability rights.

It has gotten to the point where I am almost unable to turn on the television without happening upon a program or movie that includes a disability—related theme. A fairly recent compilation that attempts to be comprehensive in listing and providing short descriptions is Lauri Klobas's *Disability Drama in Television and Film* (Jefferson, N.C.: McFarland, 1988). If there were to be a second edition, I have the sense that the book's size would double, in just ten years. This is a commentary on how common disability themes have become in the most recent of times.

The closest comparisons to Hevey's analytical forays about disability and society in the United States come from Frank Moore. I often begin presentations with the following excerpt from his long prose poem, "Out of Isolation:"

I lie here in my universe of the mat, my bed. I always have been here lying in my universe forever, forever. My mat, my pillow, my sheet, my blanket…for countless force-fed meals, enemas, baths, shaves, haircuts, pissed-on sheets…many many harsh-lighted days, many, many semi-dark nights. Outside my universe there are bony fingers, blotch-skin creatures. Sometimes they invaded my universe…the sickly-sweet smelling ones. They "take care of me"…they handle me like they handle my pillow. Their voices are high, loud, flat. Sometimes they lie on beds beside mine, moaning and crying for alone many many, then they get quiet and others of them carry the still ones away. There are always new ones, but they are always the same. There are different bony fingers who invade my universe, who strip me, probe me stretch me until it hurts…do strange things to me like rubbing ice on my body then brushing me hard. They talk to me in funny ways…loud and flat. They say, "We are doing this for your own good." They don't think I understand what they are saying. I don't understand most of their words. But I understand enough, I understand I am not a Mister, a Mrs., a Miss, a Nurse, a Doctor. I understand I am not bony fingers. They can keep their universe of bony fingers. I am not going out of my universe of the mat. I understand enough. A long long, when I cried out, they made me numb. I do not like being numb. In my universe of the mat, I am not numb. But they said crying out was not "appropriate behavior". I do not think appropriate behavior is good.

Everything that is not appropriate behavior makes me feel. But I understand enough to stop crying when the bony fingers are around. Stop making any sound, any move when they are around. They stopped making me numb.

I understand enough. I discovered a way of rubbing myself that makes me warm, makes me feel good. Bony fingers slapped me away from feeling good. Not appropriate behavior. I understand enough. I do appropriate behavior in the harsh light when they are around. I am still, quiet. In my universe of the mat. I do not even look into their world. I am busy creating within me. But when the harsh light goes and the semi-darkness comes...when only the still or moaning bony fingers are around...I move, I laugh, I cry, I rub my body and good feeling comes. Not so loud or so much that the harsh light, the bony fingers, and their numbness come back. But just enough. And by rubbing, I know I am not bony fingers.[13]

When I finish I describe Frank as a performance artist from the Berkeley, California area who has significant cerebral palsy and for much of his life has been described as non-verbal! In a lecture given at New York University in the 1980s and then published as *Art of a Shaman* (Berkeley: INTER-RELATIONS, 1990), Frank says, "It was just my luck to be born into the long tradition of the deformed shaman, the wounded healer, the blind prophet, and the club-footed 'idiot' court jester."[14]

Moore, the painter and artist, might appreciate two books of photography. The first is Lydia Gans's *To Live with Grace and Dignity* (Horsham, PA: LRP Publications, 1994). Gans has been taking pictures of individuals who use Personal Assistance Services (PAS) for many years and has compiled a book that presents twenty-three stories of work, friendship, and living with a disability or with someone with a disability.

In a similar vein, Suzanne C. Levine journeyed to Project Projimo in rural Mexico, a community of people with disabilities who live and work together. Her book *Volver a Vivir/Return to Life* (Berkeley, CA: Chardon Press, 1996) includes narratives written in Spanish (and later translated into English) by those she photographed.

Many individuals have also dramatized their lives with disabilities through poetry. Some of the best full-length publications are Karen Fiser's *Words Like Fate and Pain* (Cambridge: Zoland Books, 1992); Laura Hershey's *In the Way, Adapt Poems* (Denver: Dragonfly, 1992), *On the Lawn: Nairobi Women's Conference Poems* (Denver: Dragonfly, 1994), and *Dreams of a Different Woman: New Poems by Laura Hershey* (Denver: Dragonfly, 1994); as well as Mary McGinnis's *Listening for Cactus* (Santa Fe, NM: Sherman Asher, 1996). I am also partial to my own *Pain, Plain—And Fancy Rappings: Poetry from the Disability Culture* (Las Cruces, NM: Institute on Disability Culture, 1995) and *Voyages: Life Journeys* (Las Cruces, NM: Institute on Disability Culture, 1996).

In addition to Jane Field, some of the best singer-songwriters are England's Johnny Crescendo, Mike Higgins, and Ian Stanton; and from the U.S., Elaine Kolb, Jeff Moyer, and Blue O'Connell. All but Crescendo sing in a folk style. Like his adopted name implies, Crescendo rocks. Field, as her lyrics demonstrate throughout this article, fills her music with humor.

Three articles about theater and dance are good examples of disability culture in those areas. Actress Victoria Ann-Lewis wrote "The Secret Community: Disability and the American Theater," *Disability Rag & Resource*, 16 (5), (Sept./Oct. 1995); Eric Backman explores a variety of art forms and disability culture issues in "Amazing Grace," *MAINSTREAM: Magazine of the Able-Disabled*, (Aug. 1994); and dancer Charlene A. Curtiss discusses her craft in "The Integrated Dance Movement," *Disability Rag & Resource*, 16 (6), (Nov/Dec. 1995).

In recent years, videos have begun to be made by people with disabilities about our issues. Appendix (page 193) includes a list of my favorites representing various subjects.

HISTORY

Many of us don't know about our history. Not so much because we don't have it, but because until recently it has not been deemed worthy of discussion. That's changing as the following examples attest.

Edward D. Berkowitz's *Disabled Policy: America's Program for the Handicapped* (Cambridge: Cambridge University Press, 1987) was one of the first works of history to focus on disability policy and explain how it worked (or didn't work) in the United States since the early 1900s. His story is continued in Richard K. Scotch's *From Good Will to Civil Rights: Transforming Federal Disability Policy* (Philadelphia: Temple, 1984), a look at the crucial demonstrations in San Francisco and other U.S. cities in 1977 which led to the federal government seriously considering Section 504 of the Rehabilitation Act of 1973, which prohibited discrimination in government funded programs for qualified people with disabilities.[15] Journalist Joseph P. Shapiro has written the most popular chronicle about disability in recent memory, *No Pity: People with Disabilities Forging a New Civil Rights Movement* (New York: Times Books, 1993). He professes:

> The disability movement is a mosaic movement for the 1990s. Diversity is its central characteristic...In the last twenty to thirty years, little noticed ...another movement has slowly taken shape to demand for disabled people the fundamental rights that have already been granted to all other Americans.

It has led to the emergence of a group consciousness, even the start of a disability culture, which did not exist nationally even as recently as the 1970s.[16]

The following year, in *Independent Living: Theory and Practice* (Las Cruces, NM: Institute on Disability Culture, 1994), I look at the philosophies that led to the development of the independent living movement and symbolism in disability and how they impact the daily activities of an independent living program. I include a long introductory chapter about historical developments in *Investigating a Culture of Disability*.

One of those individuals who was a part of much of this history, Frank Bowe, wrote *Handicapping America* (New York: Harper & Row, 1978), which, although dated, remains a valuable tool for understanding the genesis of the disability rights movement and many of its contemporary issues. A second person involved in the making of this history is Hugh Gregory Gallagher. He has authored two excellent books, one depicting the original visitation of the Nazi horror on people with disabilities, *By Trust Betrayed: Patients, Physicians and the License to Kill in the Third Reich* (New York: Henry Holt, 1990), and the other a fascinating account of how Franklin Delano Roosevelt's polio affected him and the nation in *FDR's Splendid Deception* (New York: Dodd, Mead, 1985).

Paul K. Longmore, who uncovered the League for the Physically Handicapped, (a group that staged sit-ins, pickets and boycotts in the 1930s), also wrote "The Life of Randolph Bourne and the Need for a History of Disabled People: Review of Bruce Clayton's *Forgotten Prophet: The Life of Randolph Bourne,*" in *Reviews in American History*, (Dec. 1985), in which he eloquently states the case for a history of people with disabilities written by people who have an understanding of disability issues.[17]

A book that responds to this need is Philip M. Ferguson's *Abandoned to Their Fate: Social Policy and Practice Toward Severely Retarded People in America*, 1820–1920 (Philadelphia: Temple, 1994), which provides a new look at these institutions and the reasons for their existence and continuance. Ferguson also provides an excellent bibliography of this subject in "Mental Retardation Historiography and the Culture of Knowledge," *Disability Studies Quarterly* 16 (3) (Summer 1996), as does Steve Taylor, in "Disability Studies and Mental Retardation," *Disability Studies Quarterly* 16 (3) (Summer 1996).

The late Timothy M. Cook in "The Americans with Disabilities Act of 1990: The Move to Integration," *Temple Law Review* 64 (2) (1991), provides a superb overview of how disability history and issues fit into the broader civil rights agenda.

Karen Hirsch, also writing from a historian's perspective in "Studying Culture," *Disability Rag*, (May/June 1987), was one of the first to call for looking at disability as a culture, and in "Culture and Disability: The Role of Oral History," *Oral History Review* 22 (1), (Summer 1995), she makes the case that many historical analyses are less accurate than they might be with the inclusion of a consciousness about disability issues. Finally, two satisfying historical reflections about disability culture occur in Ruth Brannon's "The Use of the Concept of Disability Culture: A Historian's View," *Disability Studies Quarterly* 15 (4) (Fall 1995), and Paul Longmore's "The Second Phase: From Disability Rights to Disability Culture," *Disability Rag & Resource*, 16 (5), (Sept./Oct. 1995).

IDENTITY

Autobiographies are rampant in describing how someone has lived with a disability or impairment. But many remain in the genre of the inspirational—"how I overcame my disability and did_____. Fill in the blank with almost any field of endeavor you can conjure. Perceptions of disability from today's civil rights perspective remain few. Some of the best include: Frank Bowe's *Changing the Rules* (Silver Spring, MD: TJ Publishers, 1986), in which the author traces his early childhood as someone who has become deaf, but is not recognized for that difference; Anne Finger's *Past Due: A Story of Disability, Pregnancy, and Birth* (Seattle: Seal, 1990), in which a marvelous writer with a disability describes a personal evolution related to discovering her child will be born with a disability; John Hockenberry's *Moving Violations: War Zones, Wheelchairs, and Declarations of Independence* (New York: Hyperion, 1995), a paraplegic newsman's slants on life, reporting, and disability; and Jason Kingsley's and Mitchell Levitz's *Count Us In: Growing Up with Down Syndrome* (San Diego: Harvest, 1994), the story of two teenagers who, with the assistance of supportive and hopeful parents, discuss their lives with Down Syndrome. Nancy Mairs is an essayist with multiple sclerosis who takes a magnifying glass to her life and reports about it with extraordinary realism and clarity in several books including *Ordinary Time: Cycles in Marriage, Faith and Renewal* (Boston: Beacon, 1993), *Plaintext* (Tucson: Arizona, 1986), and *Remembering the Bone House: An Erotics of Place and Space* (Boston: Beacon, 1995, 1st published 1989).[18] Lorenzo Wilson Milam's recent *Crip Zen: A Manual for Survival* (San Diego, CA: Mho & Mho Works, 1993) is both a handbook for living with a disability and a reflection on doing just that for many years. In contrast, his earlier *The Cripple Liberation Front Marching Band Blues* (San Diego, CA: Mho & Mho Works, 1984) describes learning to live with disability and sexuality while recuperating from polio and maturing at Warm Springs Rehabilitation Center, (FDR's rehabilitation and vacation site and the wheel-chair-using President's most tangible personal legacy to future generations of people with disabilities). Connie Panzarino's *The Me in the Mirror* (Seattle: Seal, 1994), addresses some similar themes from a disability rights, independent living, and Baby Boomer perspective, while Ruth Sienkiewicz-Mercer's *I Raise My Eyes to Say Yes* (New York: Avon, 1989), describes in detail what it was like to live in an institution where very few people understood her abilities—and how she managed to escape. Judith A. Snow's *What's Really Worth Doing and How to Do It: A Book for People Who Love Someone Labeled Disabled* (Toronto: Inclusion, 1994), is both encouraging and instructive for assisting someone to get what they want out of life. The late, disabled sociologist, Irving Kenneth Zola wrote about coming to terms with disability and identity while visiting Het Dorp, a housing complex that provides Personal Assistance Services for people with disabilities in the Netherlands, in *Missing Pieces: A Chronicle of Living with a Disability* (Philadelphia: Temple, 1982).

Articles with similar and complementary themes include three of my own: "Creating a Disability Mythology," *International Journal of Rehabilitation Research*, 15, (Winter 1992); "I Was Born (in a Hospital Bed)—When I Was Thirty-One Years Old," *Disability and Society*, 10 (1), (1995); and "We Are Who We Are...So Who Are We? *MAINSTREAM: Magazine of the Able-Disabled*, 20 (10), (Aug. 1996). Other notables are: "a celebration of disability culture," an entire issue of the *Disability Rag & Resource*, 16 (5), (Sept./Oct. 1995) devoted to this theme; Gene Chelberg's and Sue Kroeger's "Tenets of Disability Discovery," *Disability Studies Quarterly*, 15 (4), (Fall 1995); Carol J. Gill's "Comments on Disability Culture," *Disability Rag & Resource*, 16 (5), (Sept./Oct. 1995); and "A Psychological View of Disability Culture," *Disability Studies Quarterly* 15 (4), (Fall 1995); Harlan Hahn's "The Los Angeles Uprisings of 1992: A Disability Perspective," *Disability Studies Quarterly*, 13, (1), (Winter 1993); Dianne B. Piastro's "Identifying with our culture—ourselves," *Disability Rag & Resource*, 16 (5), (Sept./Oct. 1995); and Cheryl Marie Wade's "Creating a Disability Aesthetic in the Arts," *Disability Rag & Resource*, 15 (6) (Nov–Dec 1994), and "Culture Rap: Why Do We *Need* a Culture?" *Disability Rag & Resource* 17 (3) (March/April 1996).

I would be remiss not to include some of the finest fiction about disability in this section, including Patricia Armstrong's *Kate* (Toronto: Harlequin, 1995), a romance novel about a heroine who, like the author, has Myasthenia Gravis; Andre Dubois's *Dancing After Hours* (New York: Knopf, 1996), a collection of short stories, many of which feature characters with disabilities, in particular two protagonists whose disabilities are essential to their stories; Anne Finger's collection of short stories, *Basic Skills: Stories by Anne Finger* (Columbia: University of Missouri Press, 1988); and her novel, *Bone Truth* (Minneapolis: Coffee House Press, 1994), the second novel of which I'm aware written by a person with a disability focusing on disability themes from a rights perspective, following Jean Stewart's *The Body's Memory* (New York: St. Martin's Press, 1989).

Many anthologies over the past decade or so have proven to be some of the most fruitful sources of discovering information about all of these subjects in a variety of formats. One of the first, and still one of the best is *With the Power of Each Breath* (Pittsburgh and San Francisco: Cleis Press, 1985) edited by Susan E. Browne, Debra Connors, and Nanci Stern. A more recent excellent compilation from England *"What Happened to You?" Writing by Disabled Women* (New York: New Press, 1994) is edited by Lois Keith. Harilyn Rousso, Susan Gushee O'Malley and Mary Severance, edited *Disabled, Female and Proud: Stories of Ten Women with Disabilities* (Boston: Exceptional Parent Press, 1988), a wonderful collection about girls and young women with disabilities. Cheryl Marie Wade has edited two of the best collections of writers' and artists' work in *Close to the Truth* (Berkeley, KIDS Project, 1989) and *Range of Motion: An Anthology of Disability Poetry, Prose and Art* (Albany, CA: Minuteman, a KIDS Project/Squeaky Wheels Press, 1993). Mary E. Willmuth and Lillian Holcomb, in *Women with Disabilities: Found Voices* (New York: Harrington Park Press, 1993) have assembled an anthology, which combines scholarly and popular voices. Irving Kenneth Zola, editor of *Ordinary Lives: Voices of Disability and Disease* (Cambridge: Applewood, 1982) includes fiction, nonfiction, and poetry in a more consistently interesting way than the more well known Vassar Miller's editing of *Despite this Flesh: The Disabled in Stories and Poems* (Austin: University of Texas Press, 1985).

CONCLUSION

Unlike the previous sections, I did not give this one a title analogous to a stage in human development. This is because I think we are, and will remain, in adolescence for the foreseeable future, while we continue to sift through the various characteristics and debates about the Disability Culture Movement.

No one questions the idea that disability may be perceived in different ways depending upon what culture a person is born into. The most comprehensive endeavor to look at disability in this way comes from Benedicte Ingstad and Susan Reynolds Whyte, editors of *Disability and Culture* (Berkeley: University of

Berkeley, 1995), an anthropological compilation that focuses on how disability meshes with various societies throughout the world.[19] Although the concept of disability culture does not emerge in this book, it has been anthropologists who have articulated the most vocal disagreements with this notion.

Robert Murphy was an anthropologist who became disabled through illness and described his experience in *The Body Silent* (New York: Henry Holt, 1987). Although Murphy found much to dislike, indeed, even hate, about his disability, he also managed to acknowledge the disability rights movement and its necessity. I have described elsewhere my feeling that Murphy's place in the context of the evolution about our thinking regarding disability reflects his own notion of disability as liminal—for Murphy, the man, it is an intermediate stage between life and death, for Murphy, author and observer, it is an intermediate stage between something horribly disabling happening to someone and disability as something that happens and can have positive or negative ramifications, depending upon how the individual chooses to respond.[20]

One of Murphy's students and colleagues, Jessica Scheer, has been most eloquent in voicing concerns about a culture of disability. She wonders if such a culture would not be counterproductive and separatist in "Culture and Disability: An Anthropological Point of View."[21] I argue that rather than being separatist, disability culture is a way to become integrated with other segments of society. If neither people with disabilities nor nondisabled people are able to view disability with any kind of realism, then how can we expect either group to truly integrate? I don't believe it is possible. The Disability Culture Movement's recognition of our history and identity is the most important recent development in our pursuit of being valued in society.[22]

Truthfully, it does not matter what we think about the concept. The Disability Culture Movement is alive and well and continues with or without any one person.

I conclude as I began; with Jane Field's wit and wisdom:

> Disabled is the better way to be.
> With all these benefits and perks that's
> How the system works
> Oh, don't you wish that you were just like me?
>
> Oh the fishing is free with your disability
> You don't need a licence like the rest.

Movies are half the price, well isn't that nice?
And the parking spots are nothing but the best!

PART IV
Profiles

DEATH AND LIFE

[Lillian Gonzales Brown and I co-wrote this September 1995 *MAINSTREAM* article about our friend and colleague, "danny," with lettering he insists on, Blake.]

It's time to talk about death. Not only the sad and unexpected deaths of our heroes, role models, and friends like Ed Roberts, Irv Zola, or others of the currently aging crip generation, but the messy reality of living with disabling conditions that lead to the inexorable reality of life's end.

Two years ago we entered a very quiet Tucson, Arizona house. A hospital bed dominated the living room. On it lay a gaunt, dying man. Steve knew him only as Lew, the partner of Lillian's friend, Dan. We spent a couple of hours with Lew and Dan and then went on about our lives. Days later Lew died—another casualty of the AIDS virus.

Since then, danny Blake has become a friend to both of us. We've gotten together many times, but it is never enough. He, too, is dying of AIDS.

danny's death will be a tremendously sad occasion for many people. For others it will pass unnoticed. But danny, like Ed, Irv, and so many others must be remembered—for their remarkable lives and heart-wrenching deaths.

danny stands about six feet tall, with shimmering brown hair, a mustache, and glowing eyes. He moves gracefully, sometimes slowly, with the caution of someone who has lived a lifetime with cerebral palsy (CP). His speech can be a bit difficult to understand—a characteristic exacerbated with the advancement of AIDS.

His life mirrors that of many of us with disabilities, who convey only a part of ourselves to the world-at-large, while clinging to an inner self few outsiders would recognize.

danny volunteered for Tucson's Cerebral Palsy (CP) Foundation, earning a reputation as a fundraiser extraordinaire, once raising half-a-million dollars at a society gala. But he lived much of his life in secret.

danny closeted his homosexuality from employers, co-workers, and the community. In 1994, the CP Foundation wanted to honor danny by changing its name to the Blake Foundation. When approached with this idea, danny assented only if the Foundation would willingly and publicly acknowledge that he was gay and had AIDS.

They agreed.

What qualities did danny possess that enabled him to come out of the closet so thoroughly that a traditionally staid bureaucracy like a CP Foundation would willingly associate itself with a gay man with AIDS? Steve sat down with danny on March 30, 1994, and turned on the tape recorder to find answers to these questions.

danny's saga began in Ohio in 1950. In timelessly classic fashion, his family delivered the mixed message that God created him with cerebral palsy for a special reason, but if he believed in God, a cure would occur. Taken to numerous revivals, danny rebelled at the young age of six. He walked out of a revival tent never to return.

danny's early education involved both a special school and an Ohio country school. He was the only person with a disability in the entire system. He endured being teased and beaten, then accepted. danny speculates that initially he may have been feared as different, but as he became more familiar he seemed less scary.

As a college student at Arizona State University danny intended to become a lawyer. During his sophomore year, his advisor unequivocally informed him that his goal of law was unrealistic because his speech was unintelligible. That very day danny switched his major to social work, where he became so successful he earned a full scholarship to attend graduate school at the University of Chicago.

In the Windy City, danny first acted upon his homosexuality. Within six months of coming out he lost sixty pounds and for the first time in his life became proud of his appearance. After graduate school, danny headed for San Francisco's gay Mecca, unaware of the area's emerging status as a home of disability rights.

danny arrived in 1977. While Ed Roberts, Judy Heumann, and hundreds of others staged a sit-in at the federal building demanding issuance of 504 regulations, danny survived for months cleaning houses. No one wanted to hire a person with CP.

He finally obtained a case manager position at San Francisco's CP Foundation. He describes this job as the beginning of his own disability enlightenment. The job also gave him an opportunity to combine his knowledge with his compassion.

Awareness of his own sexuality, heightened from his Chicago experiences, helped danny to identify a pervasive denial of sexual awareness within the CP Center. During his lunch hours, evenings, and weekends, he began to spend time with individuals and groups to discuss sexual issues and identity.

The response was so positive he volunteered to teach a course on human sexuality. About this time Lillian met danny. He saw within her someone whose potential was untapped. He suggested they co-teach a class on sexuality to people with significant disabilities, including mental retardation. Lillian's career evolved from this modest beginning to earning an international reputation in disability rights after working with Berkeley's Center for Independent Living, Planned Parenthood, the World Institute on Disability, the Institute on Disability Culture, the University of Hawai'i, and numerous international organizations.

During the 1980s danny experienced exhilarating career advancements, and social successes. He also began a life partnership with Lew. In the mid-1980s Lew retired, after many years with the Oakland Tribune, and the couple relocated to Tucson.

Lew intended to pursue his dream of becoming a realtor in the Arizona desert. That never happened. Shortly after their move Lew acquired a seemingly undiagnosable illness and quickly became too sick to work.

danny found employment at the University of Arizona Medical Center. Unlike San Francisco, Tucson did not seem to be hospitable to coming out as a gay man. danny kept his gay lifestyle secret from his new colleagues and community.

Caring for Lew became a lonely job, hidden from his co-workers, unmentionable in his new volunteer activities, and still unidentifiable. The couple finally decided to return to San Francisco to see if they could find a diagnosis. They did. Lew had AIDS.

They returned to Tucson. danny still cared for Lew mostly in silence. Although he belonged to the gay and lesbian community, danny did not participate openly for fear of losing his job.

Lew, almost until the day he died, refused to recognize the seriousness of his illness or his impending death. During these years, while more than one hundred friends succumbed to the AIDS virus, danny still found time and energy to volunteer with the CP Foundation and counsel youngsters with CP.

Today, many of his closest friends are near death. His own illness rapidly advances. Yet danny talks about AIDS as a positive aspect of his own life and community.

AIDS has mobilized the gay/lesbian community to work toward attaining civil and human rights. It has forced danny to slow down. He knows limited time remains. Still, he wants to have an impact, but it has become much more urgent to him to save his energy for himself and his friends—to make a personal, rather than a social, difference.

The Blake Foundation is not only a Tucson institution but also a testament to an individual whose unconditional love and constant presence has quietly, but firmly, enriched many lives.

danny is an unsung hero, not interested in public acknowledgement. And that's a shame. Because he serves us all. danny faces death with the same forthrightness he has demonstrated in life. He's combined joy and sadness, sharing his ups and downs living and dying with AIDS, just as he has done living with a disability in an ableist world, and living as a gay man in a closeted society.

We all have enormous tasks ahead. We constantly have to talk about living with disabilities in a way that enables the public to know we value our lives. We cannot discuss our lives with integrity unless we are also willing to confront our deaths. Perhaps that is danny's quietly thunderous legacy for us all.

POSTSCRIPT: Thanks to the AIDS cocktail, danny still lives.

MY BEST FRIEND

[In the mid-1990s publishers of the *Chicken Soup for the Soul* series notified disability publications about plans to publish a volume of disability stories. A firestorm of controversy ensued in the disability rights community. People with disabilities from all over the country discussed whether our stories seemed appropriate for the kind of smarmy, heartwarming tales included in the *Chicken Soup* books. I wrestled with the dilemma of not wanting my writings to be turned into insipid tales, but believing as a writer I might have an obligation to instill my kind of activism into this publication. I corresponded with several other writers who understood both disability rights and publishing. One, in particular, helped me arrive at a decision. I wrote and submitted a story I felt fit the framework of these books while remaining true to my life. I received an email notice that this essay made it to the next-to-final level. Then, I never heard from anyone again. As far as I know, the *Chicken Soup* book about disability never appeared, at least in part, I would guess, to the kind of publicity the request for stories generated. A few years later, while surfing the Internet I discovered this story had been lifted from somewhere and placed on a website without my knowledge. This is the first version I've published.]

Have you ever wanted a friend who would follow you everywhere? A friend who would go anywhere with you? A friend who would follow you to the moon and back if asked? I have such a friend. No matter where I go my friend follows. Such a friend can be annoying at times, in other instances gratifying.

My friend sometimes brings frustrations. Not everyone is enamored with my friend.

Sometimes, going places with my friend is like conspiring to find color in a black and white photograph. Many times, people simply do not understand my friend, and they want us both to leave.

There are times when I wish to travel alone. My friend allows no such rebellion. We stick together.

We have had our difficulties. But we remain buddies.

My friend is like a shadow. No matter where I go my friend comes with me. Unlike a shadow, my friend seldom disappears. Such loyalty is mesmerizing.

Is there any wonder I call my companion my best friend? I'll call my friend Shadow, until I reveal my companion's identity.

Shadow does not leave home without me. Shadow is charitable. Shadow would sacrifice limbs for me, losing an arm or a leg would mean absolutely nothing to Shadow.

Shadow often draws people into conversation. We are asked how we can stand to remain together so much of the time. People wish to know how we get on so well.

Curious on-lookers stop us in the street to inquire about our partnership. We always attempt to be courteous, but, as you can imagine, such a consistent strain takes its toll. From time to time we forget to be pleasant and rudely offend our questioners.

Shadow is flexible. Sometimes I can no longer tolerate Shadow's companionship. I am something of a loner and Shadow gets on my nerves.

There are times when I simply must exclude Shadow. Do I hear a complaint? Absolutely not. Shadow does what I ask without question or protest.

Shadow is trustworthy. I have never been let down by my companion.

Shadow does not argue. Shadow does not whine. Shadow does not disagree.

Shadow is not completely obeisant. If there is something I want that Shadow cannot do, Shadow will not comply. No discussion occurs. We either work it out or find an alternative to the dilemma.

Shadow is a bulwark. Shadow is supportive whenever I ask.

Shadow is friendly. Shadow is even-tempered. I provide the tempests in our relationship.

I get through each day with Shadow's kind assistance. Almost everyone I know has met Shadow. Many people do not share the same positive world-view of Shadow I do.

Have you deciphered the identity of my mystery friend yet?

Shadow is my wheelchair.

My wheelchair? My best friend? Yes.

Where would I be without my Shadow, without my wheelchair?

Most likely I would be at home. Without this means of mobility I am unable to participate in most of my daily activities.

When I get in my car I go from one spot to a different destination. When I get in my wheelchair I do the same. The only difference is that my car is likely to travel farther. There is no difference in my perception of each of these marvelous vehicles of transportation.

My wheelchair takes me from my bedroom to my kitchen, and from my office to my car. My car takes me from my home to my office, and from my daughter's school to the gas station. My wheelchair takes me from one store to another in a mall, and my car takes me to the mall. If my car malfunctions, my wheelchair takes me from a non-working vehicle to get help.

If my wheelchair breaks down, where do I go?

Much of the world perceives a wheelchair as a prison. I see liberation.

Without my wheelchair I am confined to a specific place. With my wheelchair I can get anywhere I wish, with the exception of architectural barriers constructed to prohibit my vital means of transportation.

My wheelchair is personalized.

It has no legs because I chose to remove them. It has arms because I wish them to remain. Anti-tipping devices lurk in the back since I frequently desire to lean back and observe the world around me. My wheelchair comes equipped with a lifetime guarantee because in many ways it is the gift of a lifetime.

My wheelchair, my shadow, eases my life. It offers me comfort. It enables me to live the kind of life I choose. It brings me joy far more often than it contributes to sorrow. For these reasons I consider it a friend, a good friend, a very good friend.

My best friend.

MOVIE STARS AND SENSUOUS SCARS

[*MAINSTREAM* editors asked for a contribution about love for the February 1997 Valentine's issue.]

Valentine's Day, 1992. It rained harder that day in Oakland, California, than it had for fifty years. Sheets of water cascaded onto the ground. Visibility was laughable. You couldn't inch outside without getting drenched.

My daughter took the same bus home from school every day. For two months she had no problems getting home. Today, she got lost. She couldn't see clearly through the pelting storm and didn't get on the right bus. I heard the phone ringing as I came in the door. Could I pick her up at a gas station? She described her ordeal. When she realized she was in the wrong neighborhood, she knocked on several houses. No one was home. Finally, she waved a car down. A nightmare for a young teenager in a new city. We praised her creativeness and clear thinking.

A couple of hours later, we ordered pizza instead of going out for our planned, elegant dinner. When the pizza arrived our friend Ann invited the delivery person inside to celebrate with us. He looked at her in disbelief. What could anyone be celebrating on this day?

Valentine's Day, 1992. Five years ago. Seven of us gathered in our living room, in front of the fireplace, as Lillian and I celebrated the formal union of our lives together, in a quiet, romantic wedding ceremony.

Not quite a year earlier we went out for the first time. It wasn't a date. Still new to California, I hoped to make more friends. We went out to dinner. And talked with ease. Much of it about relationships. We both recently left entanglements more problematic than fun. We shared that neither one of us ever wanted to get married again. In fact, we weren't even certain we wanted future relationships. If we did get involved, we most definitely did not want to live with the other person. We were both quite clear on that point.

We talked about our dream houses. They were exactly the same, right down to living by ourselves, alone. We wanted it that way.

A month later I moved in. A year later we sat in front of the fire in our cozy living room getting married. In so many ways, we are your average couple of the 1990s, born in the early fifties. Like other Baby Boomers, we married in our early twenties and divorced in our early thirties. Between us we had one child—perhaps less than average. We both worked. We struggled to survive on the incomes we generated. We liked similar music and movies and meals. We enjoyed similar social situations.

We also differed from many of our peers. We had significant disabilities. Lillian used either a crutch or her wheelchair to get around. Born, with a mysterious, unnamed disability, her hips were dislocated and her joints hyper-elastic. She's had over twenty disability related surgeries and spent about seven years of her life in hospitals. She has plenty of scars to show for it. The arthritis that results from her condition causes her lots of pain. I relate.

My disability, Gaucher Disease, a genetic, metabolic condition, showed up first when I was six. An enzyme that breaks down a fatty cell is lower in content in my body than typical. The cells that aren't eliminated wreak havoc throughout my body. I have broken just about every bone you can imagine. Some of them often.

Pain and disability are part of our everyday lives. Movement of any kind is often a challenge. When Lillian moves she will sometimes come to a complete stop. All she has to say to me is "my ankle." I wait. I know that eventually the ankle will do whatever it must, and she will be able to move again. Other people are startled. Why don't I do something? What can they do? People want solutions. We are much too hurried to await the rhythms of our bodies. We, too, are impatient. But we also know there is nothing to do but wait. So we do.

This dissonance impacts every arena of our lives. Sometimes, more often as we age, sexual contact presents difficulties. Which is unfortunate because Lillian is one of the sexiest people I know and easily the most compelling, desirable lover I've had.

When we make love, in whatever fashion, she is all there, and I have learned things about myself that I never knew before. How sensitive my nipples are. How exquisite it feels to have her fingers, her tongue, playing with their points.

Although I'm the writer, it's ironic I'm the one writing this article. She's the expert. She's the one who has taken courses on sexuality and disability and taught it all over the world.

One exercise she does is to ask an audience to imagine their perfect lover. How tall? How short? How round? How narrow? What is the color, texture, length, feel, and smell of hair? Is their face narrow or round? What color are their eyes?

Are their eyebrows thick, thin? What is the shape of their ears? She continues working down the body in similar fashion. She gets very specific and often shocks people when she asks them to imagine their lover's pubic hair and genitalia. Is the hair thick or thin? Coarse or smooth? If it's a man, is the penis long? thick? circumcised? If a woman, are the walls of the vagina large? small? Is the hair neatly shaved and groomed? Untouched? She continues asking specific questions down onto the toes. When she finishes people have a specific fantasy image of a physically perfect lover. She then asks the audience to think about how many people they have been attracted to who fit their description of their imaginary lover? Usually not too many. These days she uses me as an example to say that she never thought she would be attracted to a tall, slender man. My own fantasy lover has always been a woman with red hair, yet I've only dated one such woman in my life.

Our images of perfection come from magazines, books, movies, and television that are themselves fantasies. How many of us have seen our movie screen idols up close? If you have you know most of the time they do not meet their own screen image of perfection. Somehow we forgot about tricks of make-up, photography, editing, brushovers, and all kinds of techniques that make us look different than reality. Yet these figures of make-believe become our sexual icons.

People with disabilities who have obvious and subtle differences from our movie star fantasies often feel left out in the cold when it comes to looking and feeling sexy.

I sometimes ask for positive and negative stereotypical descriptions of people with disabilities when I conduct training workshops. I get long lists. Most often, sexuality is not on either list, until I ask about it. We have bought into stereotypes that we are asexual or hypersexual, but very often we forget to think of ourselves as sexy.

Many of the most attractive, sensual people I know are ones with disabilities. I think of the woman I once longed for. She had gorgeous brown hair with lots of curls. A curvaceous body. The fact that she was paralyzed made no difference. After months of working up the courage I finally asked her out. We met for dinner. I was ecstatic. We seemed to have a good time. As we said goodnight I asked her out again and she agreed. She never showed up for that second date. In fact, she didn't remember it. As it turned out, she was probably drunk or drugged the whole time we were out. She barely recalled we had a date. I still found her physically attractive, but I no longer had a desire to date her. Her disability didn't get in my way. Her lifestyle did.

I share this story because what it says to me is that people with disabilities are like everyone else when it comes to love. We all need and want it. We search for romance in a variety of ways. Sometimes it works; sometimes it doesn't.

Disability, in and of itself, is neither a deterrent toward sexual longing nor any kind of automatic repellent toward prospective suitors. People with disabilities, like everyone else, desire romance and love, touching and feeling. Some people, I suppose, would be less surprised to discover we are sexual and romantic beings than they would be to consider us desirable. But if we would spend a moment to think about standards of beauty we would realize they change drastically from generation to generation, society to society, or culture to culture. In late nineteenth century America, for example, a beautiful woman was generally far heavier than today's slender models. Clothes, hairstyles, skin tones, and other characteristics of beauty have changed often during my relatively short life span.

Some individuals with disabilities exude sensuousness and sexual desirability more than their nondisabled counterparts. Some don't. Just like intelligence, athleticism, creativity, and other human characteristics.

About a year ago I met a woman at a workshop. Shortly afterward, we met again at a national conference. One of the highlights of this annual conference is a dance. As someone who loves to dance, I make it a point to attend the event. This woman was also there. It was her first experience among a lot of people with disabilities in such a social situation. She concluded after her evening there that people were looking to score just like in any other social situation. She also noticed the dynamics you see everywhere else: sometimes people were mutually attracted; sometimes they were not. But there were a lot of different people on that dance floor and in that room with a lot of diverse disabilities who had no trouble projecting themselves—or being perceived—as highly desirable—and desired—sexual human beings.

The stereotype of people with disabilities is that we are weak and dependent creatures. Those of us who live with disability know this to be untrue. The opposite is more often the case. We are strong, fiercely independent beings. We have had to be to survive in this hostile environment we find ourselves.

This holds true in love and sexuality as well. When Lillian does trainings in sexuality, she describes sexual pleasure and numerous ways to attain it. My favorite story is about a person with paralysis who has an orgasm when stimulated on a sensitive spot on his elbow. His elbow? Yes, we have all kinds of erogenous zones. Most of us just don't know how to find nontraditional ones. Like much else with disability, it's a matter of experimenting until we find what works.

Isn't that what sex, love, romance, and life are all about?

THE CURB RAMPS OF KALAMAZOO: DISCOVERING OUR UNRECORDED HISTORY

[Many disability rights activists in the United States have learned that the city of Berkeley, California hosted a series of firsts: the first Disabled Students' Services Program; the first Center for Independent Living; the first city-wide program for curb cuts. In learning, researching, and uncovering disability rights history, I've learned that these "firsts" cannot be as easily delineated, as we once believed. One example is Threshold, the Finnish independent living center, began the same year as the Center for Independent Living in Berkeley. I learned quite by accident that the same applied to curb cuts. This story of learning about, investigating, and then writing about a series of 1940s curb cuts appeared in the Summer 1999 *Disability Studies Quarterly*.]

"Friday, April 25th, 1997, a ceremony in downtown Berkeley commemorated the 25th anniversary of the first curb ramp for the disabled. 'It's the slab of concrete heard round the world,' according to Gerald Baptiste, Associate Director of Berkeley's Center for Independent Living, noting the curb ramp is believed to be the predecessor of millions of similar ramps that have been built throughout the world to enable wheelchair users to utilize sidewalks, businesses, parks and other public facilities."

When I read the preceding e-mail message in the spring of 1997, I had only recently become aware that this bit of lore from disability rights mythology was myth indeed. In January 1997, Lillian Gonzales Brown and I had the honor of being guests on the first syndicated version of On a Roll, a radio talk show about life and disability. The broadcast originated in Phoenix and was simulcast to Tucson and Hays, Kansas.

I called my parents who now live in Tucson to tell them about the show. After the broadcast, they called to congratulate us on the fine job we had done (what else would they do?), but then said they thought we should know we were wrong in stating that Berkeley had been the first city to implement curb cuts. In fact, they stated that my hometown of Kalamazoo, Michigan, had installed curb ramps in the 1940s—and the man responsible was still alive, so why don't I give him a call?

I knew that Kalamazoo was the birthplace of the outdoor mall, but curb ramps? A few weeks later I did call the man my parents suggested. His is a fascinating story, reminiscent of more familiar ones of our contemporary leaders. His story is only one of a legion of heretofore-unrecognized pioneers. The purpose of this tale is to transform an unknown episode into a part of our history.

Jack H. Fisher was born on Sept. 17, 1918, in Kalamazoo, to Herman Fisher and Rose Gerber Fisher. Herman, the son of German immigrants who arrived in the United States when he was six months old in 1890, became President of Fisher-Graff Iron and Metal Corporation. Rose grew up in Chicago with parents who had emigrated from Poland around the same time as her future husband. After their marriage, they resided in an area of Kalamazoo called Washington Square, a religiously and ethnically diverse section of newly constructed middle class homes. Jack's parents would not permit him to cross the street as a pre-schooler. That did not prevent him from meeting all his neighbors on the square block he could traverse. An outgoing child, Jack made it a point to visit every home even before starting kindergarten. He discovered that two languages were spoken in these homes, just as in his own, and that English was the second language.

Jack collected coins and paper money. He would often take his collections on visits to neighbors and request help in assembling them. Some would give him items from their native lands and tell him stories about them. Today he is a recognized expert and well-known author in the field of syngraphics, the collection of paper money.

Jack recalls that he learned more from his collections than in the classroom. He felt comfortable with people of all backgrounds and cultures. He spent hours in the Kalamazoo Public Library branch only a block from his house reading about diverse cultures. He also befriended several men at the post office who collected, too. He would get first hand information about his collections from them as well as from the Bank of Kalamazoo where he had opened a personal savings account. People saved letters and coins for him that looked different.

When Jack was ten, his mother insisted he attend dancing school. He did not have a great talent and at first was not too interested. Then he discovered he could perform at one or all of Kalamazoo's three theaters, which hired child performers, earn up to $20 a weekend, and have a theater social life. That got his attention and interest. He budgeted half of his earnings for his savings account and half for his collections.

An entrepreneur throughout high school, he enrolled at Kalamazoo College in his hometown as a freshman, but during his first two years he paid more attention to his business pursuits than his studies. He sold advertising for publications and established his own business of direct sales of various supplies to factories, foundries, paper mills, government units and colleges in Kalamazoo. His father eventually suggested he sell his car, liquidate his inventory and accounts into cash, and enroll at the University of Illinois, where he had always wanted to attend.

While in Champaign-Urbana he went to the International House and offered to assist students having problems adjusting to the United States, the university, or new customs. Some needed help with banking, which piqued Fisher's interest in money. He sometimes received coins and paper money from those he helped.

After Illinois, he applied to law school and was accepted at Harvard. He attended even though he had never previously been to New England. He was nine months from graduation when the Japanese bombed Pearl Harbor in December, 1941.

An injury from birth, when forceps had pushed through his head and damaged his left eye, prevented him from passing an eye exam to join the Navy. He returned to Kalamazoo still determined to serve and obtained a waiver directing a check of everything but his left eye. Unlike most of his classmates, who had received direct commissions, Fisher enlisted in the Army in 1942.

While serving in Oklahoma, he received injuries in a jeep accident, in 1943. He was sent from Tinker Field, a US Air Corp Base in the Oklahoma City area, about fifty miles southwest, to Borden General Hospital in Chickasha, which had a special orthopedic unit. Beds there were arranged head to toe so no one breathed on someone else. Patients always looked at someone else's feet. The ward he stayed on was for people confined to bed. He remained there from October to February.

Questions and concerns about disability were brought home in the ward he occupied. For over four months he roomed with over 40 non-ambulatory patients. While lying in full body cast, and traction, he leafed through other patients' medical records to remain busy. This engrossed him during the day so he could sleep at night. When he received his discharge in February, 1944, he wore steel braces from his hips to his neck, and possessed quite a bad limp.

While recovering from his injuries and learning to live with his residual physical problems, Fisher, at the age of twenty-five, returned to Kalamazoo for what he calls his "maturing period."

He would not return to Harvard Law School while the war waged on. He was determined to obtain a job in a defense industry. While trying to get a job he kept getting told that with his braces and spastic right leg he could not be hired, even for the lowest possible clerkship. Companies were afraid he'd fall and puncture a lung, risking worker's compensation claims. At the biggest defense company in Kalamazoo, Ingersoll, he knew the Personnel Director, but was refused there, too. Finally he tried the Michigan Employment Security Commission. Unable to find him a defense related job, they offered him a job as an employment interviewer.

Fisher did not want that job. Moreover, he contemplated the changes in his life. No more tennis, horseback riding, or other similar physical activities. What was his personal worth?

It was at this point the Disabled American Veterans (DAV) contacted Fisher at his home. The DAV informed Fisher they needed his help. About five hundred (500) disabled veterans had submitted claims to obtain medical services, financial compensation, wheelchairs, rehabilitation, and more. Their files were waiting to be processed. Fisher facilitated hundreds of claims between February, 1944, and August, 1944, when he returned to Harvard Law School.

Assisting others helped Fisher to recognize his own self-worth and realize he could still play a productive role in the world. Working with his fellow veterans was important in another sense as well. Fisher socialized with those whose claims he worked, and he learned to be comfortable with people with all sorts of disabilities and physical appearances.

Fisher graduated from Harvard Law School in February, 1945. Large and prestigious eastern firms generally sought Harvard graduates. Fisher's experience was different. Although he graduated in the top third of his class he encountered two forms of discrimination. Some firms refused to hire him, stating his disabilities and braces made him a poor risk for health and additional injuries; others would not hire Jews regardless of qualifications.

The Dean of Harvard Law School sent Fisher a telegram stating an appointment had been arranged for Fisher to be interviewed by a large Detroit law firm comprised of Harvard lawyers. All levels of partners interviewed him. In the conference room all the partners gathered to announce to Fisher that he met all the firm's qualifications. Despite his being Jewish they would make an exception to their policy and hire him. Fisher responded by stating that he was pleased he met their qualifications, but they did not meet his. He refused the offer.

He decided to begin his own practice. Fisher took the bar exam in June, 1945. He was sworn into the Michigan bar in September of that year and opened a small office that same month.

From his first day of practice, disabled veterans whom Fisher previously assisted retained him as their attorney. He remembers his practice looked like an emergency room, with clients using crutches, riding in wheelchairs, and using other adaptive equipment. These disabled veterans also brought their parents, grandparents, aunts, uncles, siblings, and friends. Fisher worked on all kinds of issues with them from real estate purchases to wills, business ventures, leases, marital concerns, and more.

People with disabilities who had not been in the military also sought his services. Throughout his career, about one third of his clients were people with disabilities. Recalling his frustrating experience looking for work after his discharge from the army, with six years of college, he wondered how other people who did not have that kind of education would find work? If employers hadn't been in the service, they would have no empathy. Fisher did whatever he could to place people whom he knew would work out and many people stayed with these companies until retirement.

Standard attorney fees were $5.00 per hour at this time. Fisher did not charge disabled veterans when working on their disability problems with government agencies. He assisted them to obtain employment, and with disability related marital and family problems. This resulted in about 25% of his time being pro bono. His first year in practice his secretary worked half the hours he did and received about twice Fisher's weekly earnings.

Fisher immersed himself in the lives of individuals with disabilities as fellow veterans, friends, acquaintances, and clients. He learned about problems of access, mobility, employment, the bedroom, and the bathroom.

Fisher journeyed the short distance from Kalamazoo to Percy Jones Hospital in Battle Creek (the old Kellogg sanitorium featured in the movie, *The Road to Wellville*) because it was the official government hospital for treating and rehabilitating amputees. A huge number of both above and below the knee amputees resided in Battle Creek. Many traversed the short distance to Kalamazoo for the bigger city's more active social life. It was not uncommon to see people using prostheses. Unfortunately for those going downtown, Kalamazoo's curbs were quite tall. People fell down on them, breaking stumps, and otherwise injuring themselves. Wheelchair users were simply unable to travel downtown.

Fisher took it upon himself in 1945 to get curbs cut and side-pipe rails. He petitioned the Kalamazoo City Commission and testified before them. City Manager Edward S. Clark, whose adult son used a wheelchair, understood the problem first-hand. The City Commission authorized the construction of cement ramps with safety rails in the central business district. Test ramps were constructed in 1945 and placed at the corners of three or four blocks.

The Buck-Crosby Chapter #6 of the DAV, for which Fisher served as commander from 1945-1947, monitored their usage. In a March, 1946, letter to the Mayor, Fisher stated the "ramps were instrumental in allowing disabled veterans, disabled non-veterans, aged and infirm persons and mothers with baby carriages more freedom of movement..."

He also wrote, "These cement ramps in many instances mean the difference between disabled veterans and disabled non-veterans having employment, as with the ramps a person confined to a wheel chair, on crutches or wearing an artificial limb is able to get to a place of employment unaided. The ramps thus enables many so called unemployable persons to become employable persons, and not only benefits the disabled person alone, but benefits the community at large as well."

The City Commission appropriated $680 to install 34 additional curb cuts, the first citywide curb cut program that we know about in the United States. This historic discovery should change how we describe the Berkeley curb cuts without diminishing their impact.

[While working on the book's final draft I learned of Jack's death. He will probably be unsung in the disability rights movement. Like many others before, and after him, his deeds impacted many, but will be remembered by few.]

IN FREEDOM, FRANK

[The greatest benefit of email is meeting new people. I read one of Berkeley resident Frank Moore's poems shortly after leaving California. We struck up an email correspondence and have remained in communication ever since. This version of Frank's life appeared in the June/July 1998 *MAINSTREAM*, the magazine's final issue.]

Frank Moore, an underground performance artist from Berkeley, California, who has significant cerebral palsy and for much of his life has been labeled non-verbal, is a beacon of possibilities in life and art.

My first encounter with his work came when I read the long prose poem "Out of Isolation," (quoted on pp 101–102). I contacted him, and we've been communicating ever since via letters, poems, prose, e-mail, and a variety of publications.

Frank's incredible lust for life and art has brought a tribe of people together through a variety of means, most recently through his e-salon.

A perfect example of the ideal, Moore espouses the world is changed one person at a time. I am unclear who lurks on the e-salon, listening but not participating, but active contributors to daily conversations include Frank himself, many talented artists, academics, "zine" (small press, non-establishment magazines) publishers, web site creators, an Indian chief, and even a few disability rights advocates. Many individuals are multi-talented and fit more than a few categories.

Common elements among e-salon participants seem to include desires to be creative, true to oneself, and respectful of other participants in the growing salon. The result is the creation of an amazingly supportive online community. Gregg Johnson described the e-salon in a college paper:

> "They [e-salon participants] speak however they choose on the list, they speak in poems, they rant or whine, they formulate well-rounded theoretically and philosophically stimulating electrobabble. The majority of them create; people on the list spend their paychecks mailing out their small press magazines with their print runs of 100; they write plays that 50 people will ever see; they

record tapes of their own in their bedrooms and send it to their friends… they sleep with girls or guys, and maybe vegetables if they're lonely, then they draw it or write about it, but it's not pornography."

Many people in the San Francisco area remember Frank from his 1970s entourage, "The Outrageous Beauty Revue." The group performed self-described Tack Rock in various states of undress and lit up the stage with their renditions of popular songs and whatever else seemed to fit any particular night.

Before the term disability culture attained any kind of popularity, these performances included people with and without disabilities making fun of popular culture in ways no one expected, especially from someone with the kind of severe handicap, to use the language of the time, that many people believed belonged in a nursing home.

Frank himself proudly recalls being one of the first seven performance artists blacklisted by Jesse Helms. If galleries booked Moore, they were then liable to lose their government monies because his art was considered obscene.

How did he attain the roles of guru, shaman, artist, and underground disability rights advocate he now holds?

Born in 1946, in Columbus, Ohio, Moore lived on an Air Force base until the age of eight. His father, a master sergeant, then took his family all over the United States and to Morocco and Germany before settling in Redlands, California, when Moore was 16.

With a child unable either to walk or talk, Frank's parents were advised to institutionalize and forget him. But they rebelled and kept Frank within the family home, fighting for him to be a member of his community.

As many of us with disabilities can understand, he lived the life of an isolated outsider even within this home setting. In fact, until he was 17, and invented a head pointer, he had no way to communicate beyond family members. He constantly struggled to break free from the restrictions of his body and self-image.

Moore's emerging personality fit well with the protest movements of the 1960s. In high school he snuck into a mimeograph room, with the protection of a friendly teacher, and ran off copies of a political column for an underground newspaper. In college he started doing political pranks like rolling into a Marine recruiting office to enlist and see the reactions.

In the 1970s, shortly after the intense emotions of shootings on college campuses over Vietnam War protests, Frank dropped out of college and moved to Santa Fe where he joined an art commune. There he rejected politics and turned to magic and art (in 1963 he started to play with oil paints) to effect change.

While Moore began to understand his role in life as an artist he still needed to break through the isolation of no physical contact. As a person with spastic cerebral palsy, he had little confidence in his own ability to become romantically involved with someone. As an artist, he both wanted and needed to communicate with people on an intimate basis.

In one of those inexplicable epiphanies that many of us undergo he decided that his self-image of ugliness projected into the world and contributed to his isolation. Changing his self-image, he exposed his new inner awareness of beauty to external examination and learned that people believed he actually looked different.

Moore took his wordboard onto the streets and waited for people to interact with him. And they did. He learned that if he opened himself up to possibilities, opportunities came along.

One such incident he often describes. About two years after Frank started doing formal performances and workshops, he searched for someone to perform in the nude along with him (his first nude play was accepted on a college campus in 1970, but he could not find actors) and he ran into Linda Mac, who worked in a travel agency. She was intrigued. They've now been together for more than 20 years.

When Moore was ready to leave Santa Fe, he created a performance art group that he first moved to New York City, then to Berkeley. The Outrageous Beauty Revue of the 1970s became the Outrageous Horror Revue of the 1980s and 1990s.

Moore has described himself, in a series of his own writings, as being lucky to be born an exhibitionist into a palsied body, which people want to stare at, and fortunate to be continuing the tradition of the deformed shaman.

> Primitive tribes believed that if a cripple could survive childhood, he was blessed by the gods. He was special. He was not really from this physical world. He belonged to the spiritual world, with an inside channel to the gods. He was not suited for the normal activities of living such as hunting and fighting. But everything he did or said were omens from the gods. He was taken care of by the tribe and lived in freedom.

Altered realities through warping time and body imagery play integral roles in Frank's subversive art. Caves also fill important components of the art. Time, nudity, and caves are often combined in his performances, which have lasted as long as 48 hours.

While other members of his troupe perform and interact with participants, Frank often is apart, meeting people in a space set aside as his cave. Only they know what happens.

The nudity in Frank's life and art easily offends people. Although subverting reality is a goal, he has also coined the word "eroplay" to explain the importance of nudity in his work. He describes eroplay as the activity of getting people to know one another's bodies in a fun and non-sexual way. In contrast, Moore defines pornography as sexuality without feeling.

Frank does not fit easily, if at all, into the conventional disability rights movement. But his life is a testimony to our rhetoric of independence and equality of opportunity. His catalog of successes include books, pamphlets, videos, a well-respected zine, *The Cherotic [r]Evolutionary*, and his web site, The Web of All Possibilities, which includes a new communication media called LUVER (Love Underground Visionary Revolution). At the web site visitors can enter the Shaman's Cave, see paintings and photos, link to many other sites, and keep up with current performance art activities.

Frank supports people who remain true to their vision. You might even say he supports the vision(s) that live through people. Consistent with his life of subverting traditional expectations, he is resistant to labels:

> "i agree that by accepting labels like gay artist, black artist, crip artist, woman artist, etc., we artists are playing into the forces that seeks to isolate/fragment people, to box art into neat fashionable packages, easy to identify [and once identified, thinking usually stops], into sound/image/cultural bites...i've always dodged being "a crip artist" because that limited the art. art should be free to explore anything, to use anything to reach the universals."

You can check out the possibilities at: http://www.eroplay.com or PO Box 11445, Berkeley, CA 94712.

ZONA AND ED ROBERTS: TWENTIETH CENTURY PIONEERS

[This is the story of two people who played instrumental roles in the disability rights movement of the last half of the twentieth century. They are two of the reasons why so much attention has been focused over the years on Berkeley as the birthplace of the independent living movement. I had the great pleasure of interviewing Ed several times, after meeting him in the early 1990s. In the late 1990s, I received a year-long fellowship to begin work on a biography about Ed. I conducted extensive interviews with Zona during this time. When that year ended, I sought, without success, further funds to continue research on a book. The article here first appeared in the Winter 2000 *Disability Studies Quarterly*. It is still the most extensive biography of these two disability rights pioneers.]

INTRODUCTION

I earned a doctorate in history from the University of Oklahoma in 1981. Unsuccessful in my job search, I accepted a one-year instructorship at my alma mater. At the end of that year, my department chair inquired if I would be interested in writing a history for and about a private association located in another part of the state. I grabbed the opportunity. A number of phone conversations ensued. The association's representative encouraged me to submit a proposal and then helped me refine it.

During another phone call I was hired.

At my first in-person meeting with my contact, I walked into the airport terminal using a pair of crutches needed because of a lifelong disability. A written contract never materialized. Within a week I was informed that my use of crutches caused the association to determine that I did not possess the energy or stamina to do the job.

Angry and frustrated, I drove to the local center for independent living, a community advocacy organization for people with disabilities, which I had learned about from two students, to see what I might do to rectify the situation. To make a long story short, there was nothing I could do. Although everyone, from my colleagues to the Oklahoma Human Rights Commission agreed that I had encountered discrimination based on my disability, I had no legal protections.[1]

That summer I volunteered most of my time at the independent living center. In the fall I was hired to fill a new full-time position. Since 1982 I have worked in the disability rights movement, but I have never relinquished my academic roots as a historian. I continue to speak and write about historical issues from a disability-rights perspective and disability rights from a historical perspective.

In 1990, shortly after chairing two panels focusing on disability history and culture, I accepted a job at the World Institute on Disability (WID) in Oakland, California. I knew about, and held in awe, many of the exceptional people working at WID.

They included: Judy Heumann, first lady of the modern disability rights movement, who had been a rebel since her New York City kindergarten had told her in the 1950s that she could not attend her neighborhood school because she used a wheelchair[2] and who, in the 1990s, became an Assistant Secretary in the Department of Education during President Clinton's two terms, and now works at the World Bank; Simi Litvak, world-renowned expert in research about Personal Assistance Services, (people aiding those of us with disabilities in tasks of daily living, such as getting in and out of bed, going to the bathroom, and getting to work); Deborah Kaplan, a disability rights lawyer, who worked with Ralph Nader, became a leader in innovations concerning technology and disability, and is the current Executor Director of WID; Hale Zukas, often perceived by the outside world as a quadriplegic unable to speak intelligibly, who graduated with honors from Berkeley with a double major in Russian and mathematics; and Ed Roberts, WID President, an internationally respected activist, considered to be equivalent in stature to Martin Luther King, Jr. by many in the disability rights movement.

I had not heard of Zona Roberts, Ed's mother. As I got to know both Ed and Zona I started to have a better grounding in the evolution of the disability rights movement. In December 1996, Zona visited our New Mexico home to engage in interviews for the book I hoped to write about Ed. At that time, I realized that Zona's tale was just as significant as that of her son.

A vibrant seventy-six year-old woman, whose age and gray hair belies boundless energy, Zona spent mornings ruminating thoughtfully for the tape recorder and afternoons touring southern New Mexico. During the evenings, Zona wanted to cook and play with our cats, before settling down for a quiet hour or two of reading.

When the interviews were completed, eleven hours of tape contained detailed, sometimes brutally honest, reflections about her life and times. I learned that Zona's life held fascinating detail before Ed's birth. She truly is a remarkable woman who is one of our century's pioneers and the sharing of her story will, I hope, become part of our national lore.[3]

BEGINNINGS

Howard Harvey, youngest of five children, labored in a mill near Portland, Oregon. He wooed and married Naida Post, an attractive carpenter's daughter with cultural ambitions centered on music and art. Teenage parents, nineteen year-old Howard and seventeen year-old Naida Harvey, shared the joy of their daughter Zona Lee's birth on April 1, 1920, in Portland, Oregon.

The exhilaration common to the arrival of a new baby did not last. Naida had two big problems with Howard. First, she was more ambitious than her husband. Second, she had a lifelong concern, sometimes bordering on paranoia, about contagious diseases, including tuberculosis (TB), which ran rampant in Howard's family. Worried that Howard would contaminate herself and her daughter, the couple parted when Zona was an infant.

Naida's fears were not entirely unfounded. Howard died from TB when Zona was about nine. The dissolution of the marriage might have been perceived as a portent. Howard and Naida's newborn daughter experienced a radically different childhood than we generally read about in the history books for middle-class America in the early twentieth century.

Zona's early remembrances about Naida focus on two aspects of their lives: the men they encountered and what both she and Naida had to endure to survive. In her biological family, both Zona's maternal grandfather and great-grandfather were carpenters, but they played less significant roles in her childhood than the women of the matriarchal family. Marriage was not a lifelong commitment in this family. Zona's grandmother married three times and Naida would eventually marry five times, four of those unions while Zona was still a child.

After Howard's departure, Naida at first gave piano lessons to survive, but she continued to seek companionship and security she believed would result from marriage. She got a job at the Montgomery Ward store in Portland. While working there she met Leo Adams. When Zona was about four and too rambunctious for her grandmother to supervise comfortably Naida decided to marry Leo. She viewed him as quite a catch partly because he owned a home in Portland.

Zona remembers Leo as a jealous stepfather who became abusive. She recalls incidents when her stepfather placed a pillow over her face and threatened to choke her and when he struck her at the dinner table. During a trip to nearby Boise the family stopped at a dam and Leo held Zona over the edge. Her stepfather terrified her. What others perceived as contentions between Leo and Zona contributed to the fairly rapid dissolution of this marriage.

Naida then married Bob Baring, a music teacher, from Stockton, California, who'd been married before. He was the father of two daughters. Naida and Zona joined Bob at his home in Stockton when Zona was about seven or eight years old, then moved to the San Francisco Bay Area when Baring got a job at the College of San Mateo.

Baring, an only child, had been a violin protege, whose musician friends spoiled him. He spent more money than he earned. He also had an unsavory side.

It eventually became unclear if Baring had divorced his previous wife when he met Naida. Complaints from students revealed he also was a child molester. In early adolescence, Zona, molested by a second stepfather, became bed-ridden, complaining to her mother about Baring. Naida responded what would they do without him? A doctor suggested Zona needed a change of environment so she went to live with relatives in Oregon. Her two years in this pastoral country setting freed her from the pressures of Naida's home. She recalls these years as two of the happiest and most serene of her childhood.

During Zona's Oregon sojourn Naida left Bob Baring. She got a job teaching ballroom dancing where she met George Stevens, known as Steve, an early San Francisco radical, with ties to communists in the area. Zona learned about their marriage from the wedding announcement. Steve seemed to satisfy and placate Naida. This marriage, her fourth union, would be her only long-term one.

Zona rejoined her mother, and her new husband, to begin her sophomore year of high school in Portland, where her mother and new stepfather relocated. Steve, a writer, attempted to publish a magazine.

Zona hoped to finish high school in Portland, but that was not to be. The magazine never became established and the family moved back to the San Francisco area.

Zona's independence asserted itself at an early age. Having already lived away from home Zona felt capable of living apart from Naida and Steve. She chose to attend high school in Burlingame, south of San Francisco, because she liked that community. She left Naida and Steve to live as a domestic worker with a family in nearby San Mateo while she attended school.

While at Burlingame High School, Zona played in the orchestra and participated in drama. She wanted to participate in more extracurricular activities but instead had to work.

Zona had been attracted to the opposite sex from a fairly early age, having had boyfriends in Oregon. While still in high school, Zona met Verne Roberts through a mutual friend. Their first activity, more an outing than a date, they played tennis. The 5'10" or 5'11" Verne later told Zona he liked her legs.

Verne, four years older than Zona, happily left high school to work when his father became ill during Verne's senior year. When he and Zona met he lived with his parents in Burlingame, sleeping on a couch in the living room.

Zona graduated from high school in 1938. She also became pregnant that year. They visited an abortionist, but Zona refused to abort her baby.

She and Verne married on July 4, 1938. Naida was not particularly happy with the marriage, believing Verne was not good enough for her daughter.

After their marriage, the newlyweds returned from their honeymoon in Fresno to San Mateo where they rented an apartment for a couple of months. Then Verne's parents bought them a four-room house for $2500 across from Burlingame High School and near their own home.

FAMILY LIFE

Verne's father, Walter, worked for Southern Pacific Railroad as a machinist. Verne was on the Extra Board for the railroad, meaning that when work became available he received calls to do odd jobs. Unfortunately, jobs and money evaporated during these Depression times. The couple applied for welfare.

Verne applied for lots of jobs while waiting to hear about welfare. Zona remembers this as a horrifying experience. The morning the welfare worker was due to arrive; Verne got a job at a furniture store. He made $25 a week there before being called back to work at the railroad as an apprentice. Since he came in as Walter's son, railroad cohorts looked after him. He started as a machinist, then electrician, then diesel electrician. He rejected promotions to foreman, although he would sometimes fill the position on a temporary basis.

Edward Verne Roberts was born on January 29, 1939. Verne wanted to name a son, Ed, after his best friend. Zona preferred the name Michael, but Verne's parents, who had become very influential in her life, especially her mother-in-law, Katherine, who had accepted her into the Roberts family as one of their own, thought Michael was an Irish name and the Irish were denigrated in San Francisco.

Following a long labor, Ed was born, weighing a little over six pounds. Zona remembers looking at her child and thinking he looked like a rat with dark hair. She remained in the hospital for about a week after Ed's birth. She recalls having a difficult time remaining still while in the maternity ward. She tried to nurse Ed, but had little success because of a tooth abscess that hemorrhaged. Ed wasn't getting enough nutrition. Once the problem was discovered, Ed received food supplements that alleviated the situation. The cost for pre-natal care, delivery, and post-natal care was $50. When Verne and Zona brought Ed home they put him in a bassinet next to their bed and Zona said, "Well, here we are—I don't know how we're going to do it, but we're gonna do it!"[4]

Creating family stability to avoid repeating her own chaotic childhood became paramount. Zona recognized deficiencies in meeting this goal, such as her initial lack of cooking skills. At the beginning of her marriage her specialties were jello salads and cakes. Verne's mother always had a pot of soup going, and Verne would frequently venture over there in the evenings.

Roberts' family gatherings, such as celebrations of holidays, often happened at her in-laws house, which Zona enjoyed. After several years, Verne questioned why they always spent holidays at his parents. One Thanksgiving, in the mid-1940s, Zona cooked chicken and then they went to the big football game, San Mateo High School versus Burlingame High School, across the street.

Ed was an early walker and talker, saying, "kitty-cat" when he was about nine months. He ran everywhere taking after his father who liked running so much that he once chased a dog around the block to get him back into the house. Ed constantly put his top teeth through his bottom lip while scurrying around.

A day after her twenty-second birthday, Zona gave birth to the family's second son, Ron, on April 2, 1942. He was a very blonde, gorgeous baby, similar to the Gerber baby. Ron tagged along with Ed when he went to the high school to play. One time Ron suffered a concussion when he was hit by a car while running after Ed. That was the first major trauma for either boy.

Ed began nursery school, then attended McKinley Elementary School. Still in constant motion, his motivation for going to school was the playground where he was the center of attention and activity. Ed did not sit still long enough to learn to read until the fifth grade.

Verne, fitting the middle-class stereotype of the day, spent much of his time at home in the garage fixing things, or gardening. He was well known throughout the neighborhood as someone who could and would lend a helping hand. He knew more about their neighbors than Zona did. Verne wanted Zona to be at home, perceiving a homemaker as someone who literally remained in the home. Most of Zona's friends, also married to blue-collar workers, had similar constraints.

Despite Verne's preference, Zona managed to find opportunities to become involved in her community. She would strategize ways to leave the house. Some of these activities played formative roles in her later life and career choices. For example, she volunteered for Parent Teacher Association (PTA) activities, such as teaching sex education classes, and she later became PTA President.

Their third son, Mark, was born when Ed was about twelve and Ron about nine. When Mark was about two months old, Zona, and her friend Marge Caton, applied to be census takers. Zona took the exam and got the job, but Marge was denied because she was Canadian, so while Zona went out, Marge took care of Mark, and they then split the money. This emphasis on friendship and sharing remained a consistent pattern throughout Zona's life.

The couple's fourth, and final child, another son, Randy, was born about two and half years after Mark.

POLIO

Life changed dramatically for the Roberts family in early 1953. Ed returned from a March of Dimes benefit baseball game saying he did not feel well. He planned to go out again that evening, but Zona refused to let him leave. That night, Ed came into his parents' bedroom and slept stretched out between their two beds.

The next morning Ed awoke with a fever, stiff, holding his spine very straight. A doctor came at dinnertime, looked at Ed, washed his hands, and immediately wanted to take Ed to San Mateo County Hospital. The physician believed Ed could have flu, meningitis, or polio.

Ed walked into the hospital. The doctor performed a spinal tap to detect meningitis. Ed got up once during his first evening in the hospital to go to the bathroom; two days later, when paralysis began, and included his neck and lungs, he was rushed into an iron lung.

When Ed contracted the polio virus, the family knew of only one other person who had polio, and who had died as a result. At the hospital, they could only visit Ed through the windows of his room. They were petrified about what would happen to their son.

Ed's fever escalated at the end of the week, creating a life-threatening crisis. The physician suggested they call a priest. Verne and Zona stayed at the hospital on Friday evening watching to see if a tracheotomy would be needed. Ed awoke at about 2:30 a.m., saw his parents and asked why they were still there. Verne and Zona believed then the crisis had passed and went home.

Upon returning to the hospital the following morning, relieved that their son survived, the doctor, who lacked a warm bedside manner, asked Ed's parents how they would like it if they had to spend the rest of their lives in an iron lung? Zona immediately became concerned this physician would convey a sense of hopelessness. Her fears were somewhat alleviated when the same doctor suggested putting a clock in Ed's bedroom so he would be aware of the time.

Hospital staff tried innovative healing methods, including exceedingly painful hot packs. Hospital personnel moved Ed in and out of the iron lung and eventually out of isolation into a ward with other polios, as they call themselves, of all ages and both sexes.

A new routine settled over the family. Zona visited Ed in the afternoons, Verne arrived in the evenings. He began to develop a nurturing side.

Verne had recently bought an insurance rider for 50 cents per month to cover polio for up to $5,000. When he first entered the hospital, the family waited to find out if Ed had polio to know whether he would be a public patient or a private one, covered by the newly acquired policy. Once polio was diagnosed, Ed became a private patient for two and a half months. Then the March of Dimes covered the remainder of the bills.

Medical practitioners of the 1950s believed polio survivors should do their utmost to become independent of an iron lung. For someone like Ed, whose level of paralysis meant his lungs no longer had the capacity to breathe on their own; this meant a terrifying fear of lack of air. Could he tolerate being out of the lung? Only time would answer that query.

Ed remained hospitalized for the greater part of two years. This time was crucial to see how the swelling would go down and what nerve endings would be corrected. Beyond two years there was no hope for further recovery.

During the first year, Verne and Zona took trips to the Russian River, a popular northern California vacation spot. One time they left for a week. Zona recalls she knew Ed could adapt to polio when he handled that trip. She later learned from Ed that he thought those excursions abetted his recovery. The polio had caused enough pain in his life; if his parents sacrificed their lives it would be more than he could bear.

Ed remained at San Mateo County Hospital for about nine months. Although he recovered from the initial ravages of the disease, the hospital lacked a rehabilitation program to teach him how to live with the aftermath of polio. The family learned about such a program at Children's Hospital in San Francisco. Zona arranged to move Ed. On the day of the move, they got Ed and put him in the back of the station wagon to move him from one hospital to the other. Ed became furious for no apparent reason. All Zona could imagine was that Ed felt akin to a dog going to the pound, removed from familiar surroundings. For the first six hours or so Ed spoke to no one.

Zona had to learn to drive to visit Ed in San Francisco. She had started to learn once before, during World War II, but gas rationing prevented her from completing the lessons. This had not displeased Verne. Since he liked Zona at home, the freedom she would acquire from driving did not excite him. Zona had to plan how she would convince Verne that learning to drive and being able to visit Ed herself would be appropriate. This kind of strategic planning had become a part of Zona's life. She was quite successful at it, and it would be propitious not only for her, but for Ed's recovery, and return to family and community life.

While in the hospital, Ed didn't eat well for a time. Speculation abounded about the cause, including frustration from being unable to feed himself. Zona attended a doctors meeting where she learned that with polio the hydrochloric acid of the stomach is almost depleted and digestion is difficult. But Ed's difficulty with eating was not physical.

Zona observed a private duty nurse pressuring Ed to eat. Zona spoke to a psychologist who in turn conversed with the nurse about this pressure being too intense and counter-productive. She was removed. Ed still had to be fed, but his attitude changed when the pressure was off. He later made many public declarations about his lack of desire to eat until others left him alone to make the decision to survive for himself.[5]

While Ed resided in Children's Hospital a news story about the polio epidemic included a camera shot that panned over Ed while the newscaster described him as being unable to move. Zona, watching the story, for the first time cried about her son's polio.

The hospital was filled with polios, many without families. Ed, with obvious support from home, began to think that life, as a polio survivor could be okay.

Rehabilitation work occurred during the nine months that Ed spent at Children's Hospital. He would, for example, try to feed himself with a sling but it would take most of the day for one meal. As he adapted to his condition, being fed by someone else did not seem as restrictive, when he could put his energies to alternative uses.

At the end of two years, Ed prepared to return home. The prospect terrified Zona. She feared she would never be able to leave the house again. She shared these feelings with a nurse who expressed surprise that no one had spoken with her about the Polio Foundation, which provided and paid for assistance to families four hours per day five days a week. This enabled Zona to feel more confident about the many changes to come.

First and foremost, the house that the Roberts family lived in across from the high school no longer worked. It could not accommodate Ed's iron lung and associated paraphernalia.

The family moved to a new house where they set up a bed for Ed in the dining room. When Ed came home from the hospital a fresh routine began.

POST-POLIO

The effects of the polio virus remained throughout Ed's lifetime. He retained some movement of two fingers on his left hand and two toes on his left foot. The rest of his body, including his lungs, remained paralyzed. Although he could not move, physical feeling remained.

Unable to breathe on his own for extended periods, he became, in the language of the day, a ventilator-dependent quadriplegic. Both his arms and legs were paralyzed and he required a machine, such as an iron lung or a ventilator, to assist him with breathing.

Ed spent two years attempting to breathe without the iron lung, but it was a losing proposition. He learned to breathe on his own in what was known as "frog-breathing," but it required an enormous expenditure of energy. When he finally surrendered to using the lung, he never regretted it. He felt most comfortable in this cocoon where he did not have to concentrate on breathing and could focus his attention on other matters. The lung became a lifelong friend. He would enter the lung during the evening. Once daytime returned, he would leave the lung behind, either breathing on his own or using a ventilator.

Verne's mechanical and electrical ability made life easier for the family. He also had a knack for awakening in the middle of the night, fixing, or repairing whatever needed it, and going back to sleep.

The Roberts' post-polio routine included: Verne arising early to go to work; a Mrs. Hibner arriving to provide assistance as promised from the Polio Foundation; Verne returning in the afternoon; and Zona serving dinner about 5:00. Verne often had soda crackers, coffee, or beer before dinner. This was also the time when Ed bathed. It took four people to lift him. Verne supported his head and neck, Zona his buttocks and knees, and two others lifted each side of his back.

Ed's immobility had immediate consequences even in the sanctity of home. For example, at dinner, the family's pet cat, Tigre, would often lie by Ed's head and steal meat from Ed's fork before he could eat it.

A slew of immediate, medical problems plagued Ed after his return home. His face began getting big blotches because he wasn't getting enough oxygen. He also had a cardiac catheterization because the left side of the heart had a little damage. A kidney stone caused Ed to go into shock and he almost died. He also developed a polyp behind the nose that eventually hemorrhaged and had to be packed with gauze. Each crisis was dealt with in its turn and he eventually acquired a routine of his own.

Ed, the only person in his school to contract polio, resumed his education at Burlingame High School at the age of eighteen. He joined brother Ron's class of sixteen year-olds, attending via a phone hook-up promoted by the phone company and provided by the San Mateo County Women's Club. It began with a phone connected to one room at the high school. When Ed pressed a bar on the phone he could be heard, when he released the bar he could hear, enabling him not only to listen but also to communicate with his classmates. Hands-on tutoring was provided for Spanish and biology courses.

The phone hook-up also began what became a lifetime of publicity about Ed. His picture and a short write-up appeared in the phone bill.

Zona thought she paid attention to her other three boys during these years, but remembers Ron getting caught stealing and stating he felt neglected. About this time he started playing tennis at the high school and the family bought him a membership at the country club. Ron became co-captain of the high school tennis team and also played basketball. He didn't date or drink, but played poker. The two younger boys, Mark and Randy, attended Washington Elementary School.

Verne always wanted to know where all his family members were and what they were doing. He liked barbecuing in their back yard, playing bridge, and generally being at home. He and Zona seldom went out together.

Zona still had her own dreams. Two things she always wanted to do were travel and go to college. At this juncture she didn't believe she would get to do either.

During his senior year, Ed sometimes went to sports events and wrote a sports column for the Burlingame Bee. He read with a book or magazine on an elevated bed tray, using a mouthstick to turn pages without assistance. He listened to the constant bustle of his busy home. He watched TV. Many visitors would come into Ed's open area in the middle of the house. Since he could not escape, he learned how to tune out and fall asleep, which became a lifelong habit.

Once a semester Ed's class met at his house. During Ed's senior year Zona informed him he had to attend classes once a week at the high school. Ed was terrified. He had not associated with students since he left the community as a star athlete in eighth grade. He was returning a cripple. His greatest fear was that he would be stared at. He was. His eventual response to being on exhibition changed: if everyone was going to be looking at him anyway he would be a star. But it was a while before Ed would let people see him in public. Once when Ed was about nineteen and Mark pushed him along Burlingame Avenue, a man stopped to ask Ed what was wrong with him. Ed couldn't answer. At this juncture, he had no desire to be around other people with disabilities, not wanting to be identified as one of them.

Ed had wanted to be a Marine. He was an avid gun collector who persuaded Zona to take him to gun shops. Ed even took a terrified Zona to rifle ranges where he would direct her in how to shoot. This and sports kept him in touch with the guys.

Ed graduated from high school in 1959 with a fight, at the age of twenty. His post-polio paralysis prevented him from taking either physical education or driver's education courses. His high school counselor thought Ed should remain in school another year. Zona, determined her boy would be as similar to his peers as possible, and having done all in her power to achieve this end was mystified by this turn of events.

Zona contacted the principal about the inequity of the situation. He supported his counselor. Zona next called her friend, Mimi Haas, the mother of one of Ron's friends and a school board member, to see what could be done. A school representative met with Zona and Ed at their home and asked, "Ed, you wouldn't like a cheap diploma, would you?"[6] A furious Zona got in touch with the Superintendent of Schools, whom she knew from PTA work. She also called some of Ed's teachers. They planned to advocate for his graduation at a school board meeting. Before they could act, the Assistant Superintendent of Schools announced that everyone was proud of Ed and granted the diploma.

At the graduation ceremony a fellow student pushed Ed across the stage. A big party followed at the Roberts' home. Zona believes Ed attained some of his own sense of determination from watching Zona persevere about his graduation.

Ed and Ron graduated at the same time. Ron ventured across the bay to attend the University of California at Berkeley. Ed enrolled at the nearby community College of San Mateo. To attend classes he was placed in a corset, which enabled him to sit up. A head brace came out of the back of the corset.

At first, Zona brought Ed to campus. They sought help from passers-by to get Ed in and out of the car, on campus, learning to avoid football player types who wanted to do it all by themselves, without consideration of Ed's needs. Once at the college, Ed attended class by himself, with assistance from fellow students, to traverse the numerous steps. The family eventually hired a fellow student to drive Ed back and forth to campus.

Ed spent three years at the College of San Mateo finishing two years of class-work. To complete assignments, Zona wrote while Ed dictated. Ed speculated about a career as a sportswriter. Others discussed technical writing. He eventually chose to major in political science.

Ed earned no money either in high school or at the College of San Mateo. Zona thought the California Department of Rehabilitation (DR) might pay for some books and began an interaction with that agency, which would eventually prove to be a watershed relationship for people with disabilities throughout the country. But that was still to come.

The most fortuitous development at the College of San Mateo for both Ed and Zona occurred when, in his second semester, Ed enrolled in an English class Jean Wirth taught. Jean, like Ed, knew about difference. She had been six feet, five inches tall since she was twelve years old. She became his unofficial advisor.

Jean asked Ed where he wanted to continue his education after graduating from the College of San Mateo and he responded UCLA, because there was a program for veterans that he speculated would make it fairly wheelchair-accessible. Zona was surprised, since he had never discussed this with her. Jean dissuaded him from this idea because UCLA was a commuter campus and he would have to find housing, transportation, personal assistance, and friends away from the university. She suggested instead that he apply to the University of California at Berkeley (UCB) where there was an outstanding political science program.

Ed did just that and was accepted at UCB. The application form asked no questions that related to disability. The only hint was that Ed weighed only eighty-five or ninety pounds. Zona accurately predicted that school officials would guess Ed forgot to put a "1" before the other numerals.

Ed also applied to DR for financial assistance. The DR counselor informed Ed he was too severely crippled to work and would therefore be denied services. Zona, Jean, and Phil Morse, Ed's official advisor at the College of San Mateo, then met with DR to advocate successfully for Ed.

While this was happening Jean, Zona, Ed, and Phil visited the UCB campus prior to the commencement of the school year. UCB personnel were shocked to learn that Ed was a post-polio ventilator-using quadriplegic. They were at a loss about where he might be housed. His large iron lung wouldn't fit in a dorm room. Morse contacted the Dean of Men, who suggested they see Henry Bruyn at Cowell Hospital, the on-campus student health center.

Bruyn, a physician, had worked with polios and commented that they were becoming of college age and should be able to attend colleges. He thought Ed could probably live at Cowell. Successful negotiations to do just that continued throughout the summer.

EAST AND WEST OF THE SAN FRANCISCO BAY

EAST—ED ROBERTS: Zona stayed with Ed during his first week at UCB. They interviewed personal assistants. She then returned home and came back to Berkeley about one month later to see how Ed was managing. Ed remained at Berkeley throughout most of the 1960s, but Zona had little to do with his life there. Just as she felt her role as Ed's mother demanded she be present at earlier crises, like the onset of polio and the potential fiasco surrounding Ed's timely high school graduation, she realized the time had come to let Ed make his own way into the world and for her to return to her own life.

A brief highlighting of Ed's impact while a student at Berkeley demonstrates how well Zona and the rest of Ed's circle of support succeeded in conveying to Ed a sense of power that augmented his own natural capabilities.

During Ed's first academic year, 1962-63, the same year that James Meredith integrated the University of Mississippi, he was the only student with a disability at Cowell, and, as far as we know, the first student with a disability of this significance to attend an American university. An area paper ran a story about Ed headlined, "Helpless Cripple Goes to School."[7] It caught the attention of a social worker in nearby Antioch whose client, John Hessler, had broken his neck while diving. Towering above six feet tall he was too big to be cared for by his parents and he lived in a nursing home.

He attended Contra Costa College, going back and forth to the nursing home by taxi. His social worker spoke with Henry Bruyn, after reading the newspaper story. John joined Ed at Cowell in the 1963-64 school year. He majored in French language and literature.

Bruyn began to garner a reputation for this program. Several more students arrived in 1965-66. Their arrival signaled a formal program for students with disabilities, who started to call themselves the Rolling Quads.[8] They were moved from the second floor to take over the entire third floor, with a nursing supervisor. Students had their own bedrooms. There was a common room and a dining room where the Rolling Quads met.

Ed and John roomed next to one another. They stored beer in the shower. Police once disciplined Ed for peeing behind bushes. He delighted in being perceived as a bad boy for once.

Ed's DR worker on this side of the Bay, Katherine Butcher, unlike his geographically appointed counselor in Burlingame, supported his efforts. DR paid for tuition, books, and secretarial help. Toward the end of the 1960s, Ed's DR worker changed. The new one attempted to run things herself. She told Ed what to write for his thesis and told other students what classes they could take. The Rolling Quads organized and hit the papers about this worker and got her transferred, not only flexing, but beginning to understand, their own power.[9]

WEST—ZONA ROBERTS: Zona's desire to be active away from home intensified with Ed and Ron at college across the Bay. While Ed studied at Berkeley, Zona benefited from her own friendship with Jean Wirth. It began one day when Zona took Ed to Jean's class at the College of San Mateo. While there, Jean told Zona she knew she would like her from her handwriting style. A lifelong friendship began.

Jean relinquished her teaching job to start a college readiness program and asked Zona to assist in its implementation. Thirty-nine Black students became the program's first cohort. Each student had a tutor as well as access to a tutoring center. Thirty-seven of the students stayed in the program and the high retention rate caught the attention of folks in Washington, D.C.

In the meantime, Verne Roberts expressed frustration when Ed left for UCB. Everything in their house for years had revolved around their dining room where Ed lived. Verne was uncomfortable with the change.

Zona too felt the emotional impact of facilitating the transitions of her family's maturing, and her own need to be active away from home with her husband's blessing. She had difficulty sleeping. She believed she needed someone to discuss matters with, but found it difficult to do so. Friends advised her to call a social work agency. When she called she was sweating so much the phone fell out of her hands. She began to meet with a social worker. Verne went once, but did not return.

Verne, who had been strong and athletic, began to feel lethargic during the summer of 1963. A biopsy discovered that Verne, a smoker, had lung cancer metastasized throughout his body.

Shortly after the New Year, Verne was hospitalized and the doctors informed Zona he would soon die. Verne refused to acknowledge his condition. He would not draw up a will. He even got angry when Zona visited. He thought she should be at home. Once she visited him with Jean Wirth and Mark, who was twelve. Verne was asleep when they got there. When he awoke Mark was crying. Verne looked at Zona and asked why she had hit him?

The cancer eventually spread to Verne's brain and he died in February, 1964. He was forty-seven years old. Verne and Zona had been married for twenty-seven years.

Within a month of Verne's death, Zona started going to the College of San Mateo. Since two of her kids were still under eighteen, Social Security for Survivors made it possible for her to attend school. Jean Wirth supervised her selection of classes.

The college-readiness program that Jean supervised eventually attracted many students. Chicano students began to take over. They were more aggressive than former students had been. They scared the administration. Jean was fired. She tried to return to teaching, but was no longer satisfied with it and quit. About that time she received a call from Washington, D.C., specifically because of the retention rate of students at her program, asking her to work for the former Department of Health, Education and Welfare (HEW). She moved to the nation's capital. This career change impacted Zona and Ed.

Zona finished at the College of San Mateo and applied to continue her education at Berkeley and San Francisco State University. She was accepted at both. Zona had tired of Burlingame's restrictiveness and conservatism. A prime example was that Mark had been yelled at for having a Beatles' haircut. Racial prejudice was underscored by the fact there was only one Black student at Burlingame High School, the son of a diplomat. Zona chose to move across the Bay. She arrived in Berkeley in 1967 at the age of forty-seven.

BERKELEY

Zona loved Berkeley. She thought she was the proudest student on campus. She was so happy to be there, and to be a college student at a major university; she took little note of the notorious rebellions experienced at UCB throughout the 1960s.

Her new house in Berkeley, on Ward Street, became affectionately labeled the "green house" for its outside paint job. The family's house in Burlingame sold for $19,000 and the house in Berkeley cost $59,000. Like her house in Burlingame there were always people there, including Ed, who visited periodically.

When Zona earned her B.A. in 1969, her sons gave her a graduation present of a three-month trip to Europe. Mark traveled with Zona providing personal assistance along the way to earn money. They began in Rotterdam, journeyed to Paris and Heidelberg, took a seven-day Black Forest tour on big Nort, a Norton motorbike, then on to Bologna, Rome, Venice, and Paris, before returning to Rotterdam and home.

At the age of forty-nine, Zona's dreams, that only a decade ago seemed unreachable, had come true. She got an education and she traveled. When she returned from Europe, she returned to UCB for one more year. She acquired her teaching certificate in 1970.

Zona thrived in Berkeley, but by the late 1960s Ed tired of being there. He had completed both undergraduate and graduate school, finishing all but his dissertation. Ed heard there was an opening for a temporary job in Riverside, in southern California. He planned to fill the position.

Before Ed left, Jean Wirth called Zona from Washington to share information about a bill providing a lot of money for disadvantaged students. Ten percent of the budget was earmarked for disability programs. Jean suggested Zona come to Washington for meetings about how to utilize the money. Zona had a conflict, so she recommended Ed.

Ed was agreeable and made the heady decision to travel by airplane, away from the comforts and necessities of home for the first time. Mark went with him as his PCA.

Ed experienced the first of many adventures traveling as an individual with a disability. First, no breathing apparatus was allowed on the plane, so Ed was forced to do frog-breathing on his own for hours in the air. Then upon landing he sat for more hours while personnel retrieved his manual wheelchair. Once he arrived at the hotel where the meetings were to be held, he was informed that he could not stay there because they feared his iron lung would blow up. He found another hotel.

Despite these hardships, Ed loved Washington. He met Senators and Secretaries, and he realized he made a lasting impression.

Since Ed was on his way to his temporary job in Riverside, he urged John Hessler and others to submit a proposal to HEW for funds to institutionalize what they learned as the Rolling Quads. Their first attempt did not get funded, but their second one did. It became the Physically Disabled Students Program (PDSP).

John Hessler became Director of the program. Zona began working half time at PDSP while seeking a teaching job. PDSP provided transportation and personal assistance in the home. The first group of attendants, known as PCAs, came from all over the United States. Some were conscientious objectors. At PDSP Zona drove people to and from campus, and rescued people needing personal assistance. She was on call night and day. She eventually managed the PCA services, until she left to pursue her Master's degree.

Ed did not remain in Riverside long. His physician advised him to leave because the area was harmful to people with breathing problems. He then moved to Woodside in the South San Francisco Bay area and began teaching at Nairobi College in East Palo Alto. The college attracted less traditional students than those attending UCB or nearby Stanford.

Jean Wirth had also returned to the area from her sojourn in Washington and created a new school, called Common College in Woodside. Ed taught there as well, but left in the early 1970s to return to Berkeley.

The program Ed suggested and others had implemented, PDSP, began to attract individuals with disabilities from around the San Francisco area. Many callers were not students, but there was nowhere else they could obtain the services they needed. The need to create an organization similar to PDSP, for non-students, became apparent.

Three people, all of whom had been Rolling Quads, began an organization they called the Center for Independent Living (CIL). A modest Research and Development grant enabled them to rent a small apartment and begin CIL.

Board member John Hessler became concerned the much-needed CIL would fail because of a lack of leadership. He spoke with Ed, after the latter returned from Woodside, about his fears. They agreed something needed to be done.

Ed and John met with their friends and discussed a Board take-over. Their strategy succeeded. Ed became CIL director because he did not have a job while Hessler directed PDSP.

CIL moved to an old car dealership on Telegraph Avenue, near campus. Ed convinced former Berkeley radicals to run a machine shop/van shop on the premises. CIL had to have a transportation system because people could not get around without it. Ed expanded CIL rapidly and a national, then international, reputation quickly followed.

When California elected Jerry Brown governor of California in 1974, three former law school classmates, who happened also to be Ed's friends, nominated Ed to become Director of the Department of Rehabilitation (DR), the agency that had once told him he was "too severely crippled" ever to work. Brown interviewed Ed and appointed him DR Director.

Ed brought John Hessler to Sacramento as his Assistant Director. Hessler did not remain happy in this position, after he had been running the show for so many years. He eventually moved to the Department of Health, where he remained until he died.

While in Sacramento, Ed, who had not dated until he moved to Berkeley, married Catherine McDugan, an occupational therapist. They held their wedding in the back yard of their Sacramento home.

Cathy gave birth to a son, Lee Roberts, in 1978. The delivery occurred at home so Ed could participate. He called Zona after the baby was born and said, "Bet you didn't think I'd be the first one to give you a grandchild." Zona responded, "You're absolutely right."[10]

The marriage lasted only a few years. Ed retained joint custody. He brought Lee with him on his travels from an early age. Toward the end of his life, when people from all over the world asked Ed what he liked to be called, he usually replied "dad."[11]

COMING INTO HER OWN

When John Hessler resigned from PDSP to move to Sacramento with Ed, Zona was offered the Director's position. She declined. She felt a person with a disability should run the program. She also lacked interest in that particular position and sought other professional possibilities. As it turned out, Zona did not mesh well with Hessler's successor. At the age of fifty-five, Zona resigned.

Just before Zona left PDSP she heard about family therapy. A friend gave her an invitation to a program about it at the University of California at San Francisco and Zona loved what she heard. The Family Therapy Institute of San Francisco offered a beginning course in Berkeley, in which she enrolled.

Zona applied to the Berkeley School of Social Welfare after quitting PDSP. The School rejected her because she had a job and was older. She also applied and was accepted at the John F. Kennedy School (JFK) in nearby Orinda, northeast of Berkeley, which encouraged older students. She could attend JFK on evenings and weekends. She completed all her work but her thesis. She then applied to the Wright Institute, also in the area, to work toward a doctorate, but decided against it because of the cost.

Zona did not know what would come next. She had a small pension of $100 per month and health insurance. She sold the "green house" to the same people from whom she purchased it and moved to Oakland. She had been ready to leave her formerly beloved neighborhood because the area was changing—as older people died, landlords bought their homes and turned them into apartments, altering the mood of the neighborhood and crowding it.

CIL called Zona during this transition. They had no counseling department and wanted to know if she would establish one. Zona agreed.

Watching Ed and his peers over the years speak at school assemblies and other venues, Zona observed the power not only of their presentations but also of their presence. Simply seeing someone like Ed out and about in the world had a profound effect upon children and teenagers with disabilities who had no previous role models upon which to base their future.

Knowing how potent these appearances had become Zona realized that she too was a peer. She became especially adept at working with parents of disabled individuals. She asked difficult questions, like what kinds of plans did parents have for their children to move out and live independently on their own, and did they still keep time for their own lives, including sexual activities? She shared her own experiences. She became a sought-after worker and speaker.

Tragedy struck one Saturday night in 1981. Randy, Zona's youngest son, was murdered. Remembered as sweet and sensitive, Randy drove a van for CIL, made exquisite chocolate truffles, and sold marijuana. On the night of the killing, Randy let someone in the house, ostensibly to make a buy, while entertaining a woman friend.

The little that is known about the murder comes from the friend. She related that the man Randy asked in said, "give me your bag or I'll kill you." Randy replied, "Guess you'll have to kill me." Perhaps it was a set-up. The second bullet entered Randy's heart and killed him instantly. The case has never been solved and remains open.[12]

When police informed Zona about her son's murder she was living alone in Oakland. They wouldn't leave until she called a friend. A few hours after Randy's death the house was filled with people, food, and wine. At the memorial service at CIL Zona received many condolences about her gentle son. A small ceremony was also held at Tilden Park in Berkeley after a cremation.

Zona left CIL in 1982. Some families with whom she had been working wanted to continue seeing her. She started a small private practice, calling herself a Family Disability Counselor. She chooses clients carefully. They are people who are not in great difficulty, but need supportive counseling. All come via word-of-mouth. Zona is particularly supportive to women who face the same kinds of obstacles she once encountered as an abused child and as the wife of a man who did not want her to leave the house.

TWO LIVES—TWO HOMES

Still in Sacramento and wondering what he would do after Jerry Brown's terms as governor were completed, Ed and two of his colleagues planned an organization called the World Institute on Disability (WID). Ed remained in Sacramento, trying to sell his house there, while WID began in Berkeley in 1983. This was a difficult time for him. It was not easy to find PCAs in Sacramento and now that he was no longer in state government he felt the action was in Berkeley. He finally decided to return there to join WID prior to the sale of his house.

Zona asked Ed if he wanted to move in with her, since she was alone and he was surviving on Social Security benefits because he no longer had a job. He once more moved into a living room.

Ed did not depend on Social Security for long. Within a year of his return to the Bay Area he received a call from the MacArthur Foundation, asking if he would be willing to accept what is commonly known as the "genius" Fellowship, a five-year award that is designed to enable people of great vision to pursue their dreams without money worries. Part of the monetary award went to a university or a program of the recipient's choice. Ed used it as seed money for WID.

The first WID project (a place Zona never officially worked) concerned learning about the different kinds of personal assistance programs throughout the country. WID's expansion has been rapid and involves many projects, but the initial task remains ongoing.

After a few years, Zona began to chafe from her lack of privacy at home. Ed and his PCAs had taken over the downstairs. Zona couldn't entertain like she had before Ed moved in. They had plans drawn up to expand the house, but the cost came in at $90,000 in the California real estate market that had skyrocketed in costs since Zona had first moved to Berkeley. Zona suggested Ed look for a place to live since he had finally sold his Sacramento house, but he didn't have the money for a down payment.

They decided to look for another place together and found a house in Berkeley. It had a back apartment known as an "in-law unit" built twenty years previously. Zona provided the down payment and Ed paid the mortgage on the new house on Eton Street in Berkeley. They moved there in 1991.

Zona continued with her practice, traveling when she could to visit friends and family and, when she had the opportunity, to other international destinations. Ed continued his stewardship as President of WID and became an international traveler, who garnered a worldwide reputation as the father of the modern disability rights movement.

On a March morning in 1995, at the age of fifty-six, Ed died from a heart attack or blood clot. Zona was visiting Ron and his family in Hawai'i.

Ed had just finished breakfast. Jonathan, his PCA, held up a pair of pants and asked Ed if those were the ones he wanted for the day. Ed dropped his mouthstick in an unusual way. By the time Jonathan got to him he was dead. There was no autopsy.

When Zona learned about her son's death, she immediately returned to Berkeley and opened up their house to family and friends. Their home was filled with people, food, and memories. Within a few days a memorial service occurred. So many people were expected that it was held at Harmon gymnasium on the UCB campus. Obituaries from all over the world recalled Ed's life and impact. Few mentioned Zona except as his surviving parent.

LEGACIES

Legacies from the lives of Zona and Ed Roberts abound.

Just as the breaking of the color barrier at American universities in the 1960s led to integrated campuses nationwide, Ed's attendance at UCB paved the way for thousands, if not millions, of others. In 1974, Congress passed the Education of the Handicapped Act guaranteeing an equal education for all children with disabilities. College campuses across the world are now implementing disability studies programs.

PDSP was the first program of its kind. Now almost every university and community college has a similar program, no longer restricted to students with physical disabilities.

CIL became the model for organizations of its kind. There are now more than three hundred in the United States and many more across the world.

Ed became the first person with a disability of his significance to direct a state Vocational Rehabilitation agency. Many more have followed in his wheelspath.

WID has grown from its beginnings of three people in 1983 to an organization of dozens of employees known throughout the world for a multitude of activities.

The MacArthur Fellowship has been awarded to other disability rights activists since Ed received one in 1984.

Ed's legacy may live on most fundamentally in the individuals he touched. At a memorial service held at WID shortly after Ed's death, a woman related the story of how her parents had moved to the United States from the Far East after she became disabled. She ended up in a hospital in the Bay Area wishing she were dead. When asked if she wanted anything she made a request to meet Ed. He visited. While there she related her story and he began to cry. When she saw his tears that he could not wipe from his face she realized she possessed physical capabilities he did not. Yet he was a powerful, happy man in his huge, motorized wheelchair, breathing with the aid of a respirator. She wondered why she was lying in a hospital bed. She got up. She has since become a well-known artist in the Bay Area.[13]

Her story is one of hundreds, if not more, of the people Ed touched directly. Many more got out of their beds, or their nursing homes, or their lives of listlessness, after hearing Ed speak, or seeing him on television, or reading about him in the press.

Ed changed Zona's life in fundamental ways. She reminisced that she learned from Ed about inclusiveness, disability, connections, worldwide experiences, and being brazen. She also became aware of the importance of noticing and accepting differences. For instance, if someone doesn't notice a wheelchair, the possibility of being run over by it is much greater than if someone pays attention.

Zona had both a mother's and a pioneer's impact on Ed. Aside from the remarkable life he lived, Zona believes Ed gained from her knowledge and compassion about love and loving. I believe he also gained a lust for life that he, like his mother, demonstrated for the entire world to see.

Zona continues to live in Oakland. She rents the "in-law" unit as well as rooms in the front of her house. Ron and Mark are both alive and well. Zona has six grandchildren. She was present at the birth of each of them. Her desire and success in creating in her own family stability unknown to her as a child remains her most important personal legacy. That she was able to achieve it in the face of Ed's bout with polio and its aftermath helped to give the world a human rights legacy.

My hopes are that the stories of parents who have been pioneers, like Zona Roberts, will become an everyday part of our history; that Ed's breaking of the educational barriers at an American university will be told in the same paragraph in the same textbooks with that of James Meredith, his historic counterpart; and that the struggles and accomplishments of the disability rights movement will take their rightful places in our national storytelling alongside those of the civil rights, women's rights, and other minority rights movements of our country's illustrious, but not always so magnificent, history.

PART V

Disability Rights and Culture

RETHINKING THE
DISABILITY AGENDA

[The next two essays, published in the late 1990s, reflect refinement of my thought about disability issues. This first essay began as an invitation to present a provocative speech to attendees at "Access, Attitude and Artistry, an International Festival of Wheelchair Dance" held in Boston in June, 1997. *New Mobility* published it as "Who Benefits?" in December 1997 and Frank Moore's *The Cherotic (r) Evolutionary* published it, with the original title, in 1999.]

At the end of 1981, when I attended my first disability rights meeting, a debate about language raged. The offensive words were "crippled," and "handicapped," and the new politically correct word became "disabled," which has evolved into the phrase "people with disabilities." As far back as I can recall I believed the language debate to be a vital one, not because of the words themselves, but instead, because the words represented one's sense of personal, social, and political identity.

My sense of history, combined with my notions of justice and folklore, led me to explore disability culture. Ten years ago, when I began to promote our culture, with what some might consider dogged determination, there were only a few proponents of the concept. That is no longer the case. Since I no longer feel compelled to focus each speech or article on proving there is a disability culture I have begun to explore anew my own perceptions about disability issues. In this process I realized I have undergone a significant transformation.

I returned to language. Instead of asking how our phrases reflect our group and individual consciousnesses I posed the question who gains an advantage? In simple terms, who benefits from disability? The answer angers me.

The following groups all benefit from disability: physicians and all other medical personnel who treat people with disabilities; the entire health care field, from policymakers to nursing home conglomerates to HMOs; lawyers, who prosecute and defend personal injury, custody, and discrimination cases; the "helping professions:" psychologists to social workers to special education teachers; bureaucracies, such as Social Security agencies, welfare departments, and the Veteran's Administration; industries, such as wheelchair manufacturers, vehicle modification businesses, and adaptive equipment makers; foundations, associations, and charities that raise money; researchers about (and sometimes on) people with disabilities and academics who teach and write about disability issues; people who own stocks in companies that benefit from the business of serving (or exploiting, depending on your viewpoint) people with disabilities; and myriad other groups who owe their employment to us, including rehabilitation agencies, independent living centers, arts programs, and people, like myself, who make a living consulting, writing, and talking to groups of people with disabilities.

I am not arguing that those of us with disabilities ourselves do not benefit from any of the above groups. But I am asking the question who benefits more? In terms of financial security, education, employment, physical and attitudinal accessibility, people with disabilities remain the most unemployed, undereducated, institutionalized minority in this country. Who benefits from disability? I would argue that nondisabled people reap more rewards from this classification than we do.

Now I have reached a dilemma. I am convinced it is vital people with disabilities acknowledge and celebrate our culture. But I also believe that as a group we are benefiting others far more than ourselves. How do we attain equilibrium where we are so comfortable with ourselves as people with disabilities we have no desire to be different than we are, without being continually exploited by those who ostensibly serve us?

I wish I had a revelatory answer. Instead I have more questions.

First, and foremost, why do people with disabilities, why does anyone, have to work so hard, demand so vociferously, rights that are already guaranteed to every citizen within our own Constitution? Who decided to disenfranchise us? Why does anyone let this happen? Again, who benefits? Who does not?

Second, why must we continuously demonstrate we are worthy of attention, of respect, of money? Who has decided that corporate welfare is more important than funding human rights, social service, and arts organizations? Why have we let them? Why do we continue to let them run roughshod over our interests so they can continue aggrandizement of their interests?

Third, why do we have to prove that our art is worthy? Isn't all art worthy? If not, who decides? Why do we let them? What is being attacked—the art, the artists or both?

We, people with disabilities and artists alike, have been portrayed as victims who need to be rescued. With disability, we are perceived as victims of our bodies or our minds. Artists are thought to be inept at "making it in the real world."

What would happen if all the money going to corporations and industries were divided and distributed equally to each citizen? What would happen if corporate welfare became artistic welfare?

Who would then need to be rescued?

SOME REFLECTIONS ON THE ADA

[In the late 1990s I sometimes felt like a voice alone in the wilderness complaining about the lack of enforcement of the Americans with Disabilities Act of 1990 (ADA). The ADA has been called the most comprehensive civil rights law for people with disabilities. It is. But it hasn't been enough. It leaves enforcement primarily up to individuals and allows minimal punitive damages in most cases. Since our legal system seems to work best when someone's pocketbook is threatened, this lack of punitive damages became a way for many people to ignore the law. Worse than that have been several court decisions of the past few years minimizing the scope of the law itself. They have ranged from narrowing the definition of disability to saying Internet web offices do not come under the law. In the context of this kind of evisceration of the law, this essay, originally published in *The Ragged Edge* in the Sept.–Oct. 1998 issue, now seems much less militant than it once did.]

In the summer of 1990, I made one of the most difficult decisions of my advocacy life. For several years in the late 1980s and in early 1990, I traveled several times from my home in Norman, Oklahoma, to Washington, D.C., to educate lawmakers about the pending Americans with Disabilities Act (ADA).

My brothers and sisters of ADAPT, a grassroots, street style protest organization, decided to instruct Congress in their inimitable way by crawling, out of their wheelchairs if need be, up the steps of the Capitol Building. I desperately wanted to participate in that feat.

But I submerged my own personal desire to join my colleagues in ADAPT for a greater common goal: the need to keep constant pressure on Congress over a period of several months. I knew many people would join the ADAPT rally. I decided I would not be one of them. I journeyed to Washington a week or so earlier, missing the ADAPT action.

At that time, I had no doubts that the ADA was a necessary and good law. Today I am not so sure.

I have a long history as an ADA supporter, even after my years of working toward its being signed into law. For a long time I regretted missing the signing ceremony as much as I regretted missing the ADAPT action. I had been invited to the signing but didn't go because I had a prior commitment. All my peers thought I was crazy. How could I pass up this historic occasion because of a previous engagement? For me it seemed to be at the heart of what the ADA embodied: living a life, as would anyone else. Keeping appointments, even if it meant I missed the signing, fit that mold.

Not long after ADA's historic signing ceremony, I moved from Oklahoma to California to accept a job at the World Institute on Disability. One of my assignments at WID included developing a bibliography of ADA-related publications. It was a perfect task for me, combining my commitment for the promise of ADA with my passion for research. But California seemed less perfect and my new spouse, Lillian Gonzales Brown, and I decided to move to the sunnier clime and quieter pace of southern New Mexico.

Once we landed in Las Cruces in late 1993 and began to explore the community we realized there were many violations of the ADA. We searched for a lawyer. After several years of frustration we finally located attorneys willing to pursue a lawsuit. Four of us sued a "quasi-state agency" (legal terms). I am intentionally being vague about this suit because the settlement agreement reached after one year of negotiations restricts our discussion.

For the purpose of this reflection on ADA, the actual legal aspects of the suit are less important than the stress of the process. First, we had the daunting task of educating our lawyers about disability issues in general. They were not only willing but also eager to learn; still, someone had to teach them.

While our attorneys educated themselves about Section 504 of the Rehabilitation Act of 1973, which set the stage for later civil rights laws, and ADA, we all also had to keep up with the nuances of federal, state, and local law, and activities. All the time expended upon this suit meant we weren't working—and since we only get paid when we work, we made a bargain with ourselves that our time, perhaps eventually some money (and most importantly, doing the right thing), would be worth the effort.

After an intense year, our attorneys advised us to settle out of court. Settlement means compromise and this was not the initial goal of any of the plaintiffs. But the history of courts in our locality meant we had a much better chance eventually to realize our goals through settlement than with a court date. After hours of discussion with each other and debate within ourselves, we finally decided to settle.

In this process we learned how limited the power of the ADA really is. If an attorney is not willing to pursue a remedy, where does that leave us?

ADA most often requires individual enforcement. First, an individual must be able and willing to make the commitment to pursue legal action. Then, the individual is required either to retain an attorney or to pursue enforcing the law without one—*pro se*, to use the legal term. This requires that individuals voluntarily learn as much about the legal system as people who have been educated and paid to do so. And even if an individual becomes an expert at the law there is no guarantee that a judge or jury will agree with their conclusions about the meaning and enforcement of the ADA.

Still, I cannot say that any of the above experiences themselves would have made me take the deep second look at ADA that I am now expressing. The final straw in the frustration with the law arose because of recent travel experiences.

This past May I participated on two panels in two different cities in Germany. My role was to discuss the ADA. At the first panel, in Munich, I shared the dais with four politicians, two of whom were members of the *Bundestag* (the German legislature). The audience consisted of about 70 people, most with disabilities. The organizers' goal was to persuade German people with disabilities they could effect political change. The American experience in obtaining the ADA's passage was one they wanted to emphasize.

This was great for me because I could discuss the coalition of people who got the ADA passed. I could discuss the speculation that the first George Bush had even been elected because of people with disabilities. And I could talk about some of the provisions of the law itself without dwelling on its failures.

Before I spoke panel sponsors specifically asked me not to discuss employment and ADA. The moderator said Germans think they have a much better employment record than Americans.

After the panel concluded, one of the members of the *Bundestag* corralled me to ask if employment had improved since the implementation of the ADA. As anyone who follows the statistics knows, I had to respond in the negative. She then told me she keeps looking for a country where employment of people with disabilities is working well—and she has yet to discover it.

Several weeks later I participated in the second panel at an outdoor festival in Mainz, several hours northeast of Munich. My fellow panelists were mostly people with disabilities; the audience consisted of a mixture of people with and without disabilities. The primary question I was assigned was "how has life changed for Americans with disabilities since ADA?"

Good question. The only answer I could, in good conscience, share was that the preamble to the ADA stated that Congress recognized people with disabilities as a distinct group—and that advocating non-discrimination, as the ADA does, still retains potential for long-term attitudinal change.

As I write this in July, just weeks prior to many celebrations of the ADA's signing, I wonder who—besides a slew of lawyers and disability consultants (yes, including me)—have most benefited from the law?

I spend my life promoting the concept of disability pride. The mission statement of our organization is, "Promoting pride in the history, activities, and cultural identity of individuals with disabilities throughout the world."

I re-read the preamble of the ADA and see its clear intent of providing "a clear and comprehensive national mandate for the elimination of discrimination against individuals with disabilities," and mentally leap with joy at the language.

Then I read the next paragraph whose purpose is to: "provide clear, strong, consistent, enforceable standards addressing discrimination against individuals with disabilities." Will this ever happen? I ask myself.

Almost twenty years ago I became a part of the disability rights movement specifically because of employment discrimination. I screamed foul and made a commitment to see that would not happen to me or anyone else ever again. But the ADA would never have protected anyone from the discrimination I encountered, because it was a company with too few employees to be covered by the law.

Just this week I saw a job application from a public school system that requested information about physical impairments. It was clearly illegal. Who was going to do something about it? Not me, and not the person who was applying for the job, who decided it was not worth her effort (read time and energy) to right this wrong, or even, finally, to apply for the job.

As I ponder the vagaries of ADA I am concerned about the tendency of Americans to believe we do everything better than anyone else, and about the fact that other disability communities around the globe now want to have their own ADAs like ours.

In other countries that I have visited, people say it's clear that Americans have more legal rights than they do. What is much less clear is how those rights translate into actual living conditions. Many European visitors to this country believe that living conditions of Americans with disabilities are deplorable—far worse than those in their own countries.

I am not advocating that ADA be rescinded. I am pleading we implement its intent.

Until we do, the promise, the preamble, of ADA remains its most concrete mark. As a nation, I wonder if we will ever honor that promise?

SHARED WORLD CONFERENCE III: GLIMPSES OF HUNGARIAN ACTIVISM

[This essay and the one that follows have not previously been published. Both are examples of ongoing activities in other parts of the world. Essays in this book so far have focused on the United States because that makes up the bulk of my personal experience. There is an active, thriving disability rights movement around the world. These describe two examples of that worldwide activity.]

My wife, Lillian, and I received a call in March 1998 from Patricia Kirkpatrick of Disability Rights Advocates (DRA) in Oakland. Would we be interested in participating in a spring conference in Hungary? Would we?! The prospect excited us both.

In late April we flew to Budapest (I learned "s" in Hungarian sounds like "sh" so Budapest sounds like Budapesht). Two ambulance service drivers met us at the airport. While their English exceeded our Hungarian only a little, they were very pleasant and, most importantly, knew the route to the dormitory where we stayed that night. The next day we joined a large group to travel by train for several hours from Budapest northwest to Gyor.

We sat across from two women from the independent living center in Sofia, Bulgaria, whom we met earlier that morning. They had traveled by bus for sixteen hours to attend the conference. Their organization is partially funded through the United States Agency for International Development. They gave us an information packet, as slick as any public relations material from the United States.

That morning, as we left the dorm, we also met Adam, a young Hungarian student with cerebral palsy. His use of a power wheelchair and his need for an accessible dormitory room meant he resided in this dorm, the only one in all of

Budapest with accessible rooms, even though he attended a different university. We discovered that through the auspices of DRA he had visited Berkeley. We spent some time arguing about our different perceptions of disability rights in the San Francisco Bay Area, with my own being more jaundiced.

Tour guides met us at the train station in Gyor and immediately led us on a walking tour of the old city area. We saw old cathedrals, businesses identified not only by name, but also by symbol, for example a boot at the cobbler shop, and many statues. The tour ended at our hotel.

We discovered our hosts had reserved for us a spacious room. We later learned the room was one of the most elaborate and accessible in the hotel, though each of us had difficulty negotiating the bathtub-shower. We also quickly learned that each of the three elevators in the hotel would accept only one wheelchair at a time. One was too small for some of the wheelchairs used.

When the conference opened the next morning, we learned from Pat Kirkpatrick and her husband, Sid Wolinsky, a well-known disability rights lawyer, that DRA established a branch office in Budapest in 1994 after Pat and Sid spent several months living and working in Hungary. Kirkpatrick and Wolinsky believed Hungary to be the former Eastern bloc country most open to American mentorship about innovative approaches to disability rights. They worked with Hungarian physician and advocate Zsofia Kalman to open a Hungarian office. One of their charges has been to develop an international conference. We were invited to help facilitate the third such event.

The two-and-a half-day conference began with a public meeting that included both the mayor of Gyor and the first lady of Hungary, who attended the majority of the conference. The mayor welcomed us and solicited recommendations for improvements. The first lady discussed how prominent attitudinal changes had become in the four years since the first Shared World conference. Only 44 people attended the first one. The final count for Shared World III was 135 attendees.

Lillian conducted workshops on "Peer Support," and "Sexuality and Disability," and I facilitated ones on "Independent Living Skills Training" (just as in the U.S., one participant said the most important aspect of being able to live at home was being able to find a home), and the "Journey from Disability Shame to Disability Pride." Other workshop topics included working with media, advocacy, and mental health. Board business also occurred.

I learned the biggest differences between the U.S. and Hungary are that Hungarians with disabilities are assigned one of three levels of severity of disability and receive funds based on that designation. The most difficult parts of the U.S. to explain were how our laws and regulations differ so vastly from one part of the country (or state or even within cities) to another. Finally, I learned the best way to explain the difference was to describe the U.S. as an unregulated society, something that seems hard to believe while we battle with our own bureaucracies.

During breaks and meals I socialized. In addition to the Hungarian participants there was a couple from Bratislava in Slovakia, a man from the Czech Republic, and a woman from Germany, who lived her first ten years in Hungary. People with a variety of disabilities including mobility impairments, visual and hearing impairments, and brain injuries, as well as many nondisabled allies, attended the conference.

The most striking difference between U.S. and Hungarian activists was the level of employment and education. The Hungarian participants in general seemed to have a higher level of education and professionalism than many American disability advocates. One woman was a mathematician, another a scientist, another ran her own tax consulting business. But all felt discriminated against in moving toward full societal participation.

Since 1991, these Hungarian activists, including DRA-Hungary, have attempted to pass a law covering their rights. The conference celebrated the passage of the new law, unanimously approved on the last day of the Parliamentary session, March 16, 1998, called *On Provision of the Rights of Persons Living with Disability and Their Equality of Opportunity*. It begins, "Persons living with disability are members of society with equal dignity and equal standing..." and in some ways shames American disability legislation. For example, the law calls for compliance in existing public buildings by the year 2005 and in existing public transportation by the year 2010. Like our own ADA, enforcement mechanisms await implementation. And the law includes sheltered workshops as plausible avenues for employment. The reason this remains is that the bill would not have been passed without the support of this lobby.

The combination of the new law and the energy of the conference participants led to a spontaneous demonstration. While touring the shopping plaza near our hotel following the train ride we discovered that there were virtually no accessible shops or restaurants. So putting all the workshop skills together, and celebrating the European labor holiday of the 5th of May, conference participants decided to organize a demonstration. Police granted permission for the demonstration, then participants contacted the press. We gathered first in front of Centrum, a chain department store, and asked to speak to the manager. He would not comply, so many of us in wheelchairs went over the one step into the store and started infiltrating both floors with our presence. Still no manager.

This was not an American style demonstration. After fifteen minutes to half-an-hour everyone left. Then we took numerous pictures in front of other inaccessible locations.

Perhaps this does not seem too radical, but we later learned that at the first Shared World conference participants spoke only in small groups, expressing extreme pessimism about prospects for change. That demonstrates the militant nature of the day.

Many social events were planned as a part of the conference. One was the DanceAbility Movement led by Alito Alessi, Director of the Joint Forces Dance Company/DanceAbility Project of Portland, Oregon, who had been conducting workshops for three weeks in Budapest. On his last night in Hungary, he improvised, in a limited space, to show us what the troupe had worked on. He discussed his desire to explore communication from the heart no matter how one moved.

As the conference ended people promised to keep in touch and to carry the torch of advocating for disability rights. When we boarded the train to return to Budapest the excitement of the recent days was palpable. We returned to our dormitory in Budapest to spend the next few days as tourists before traveling to Germany.

Riding in a boat one night on the famed Danube River that connects the old cities of Buda and Pest I had a chance to reflect on the conference and my stay in Hungary. The most ironic lesson learned: just like our home in southern New Mexico, Hungary is famous for chile peppers and adobe brick! Perhaps the distant east is not so far away after all.

DISABILITY CULTURE IN GERMANY

[We spent several weeks in the spring of 1998 in Germany. We sandwiched our trip to Hungary in between stays in Munich. We worked in several cities on this trip and I learned that an active disability culture existed throughout that country.]

In the spring of 1998, Lillian Gonzales Brown and I worked and traveled in Germany. I learned about many examples of a burgeoning disability culture, including musicians, writers, and theater. The German disability activists with whom we worked and talked believed that neither they nor their peers were conscious of, or ready to acknowledge, more than the wisp of an idea of a disability culture. Germany seemed to me similar to the United States in the late 1980s and early 1990s when a culture of disability not only existed, but also constantly expanded, while disability rights activists seemed cautious to assign meaning to its development.

From our home base in Munich, my wife and I traveled to Kassel, several hours north, where Lillian conducted a sexuality and disability workshop at the local Center for Independent Living (CIL). We stayed at the home of Uwe Frevert (formerly Frehse), who is well known in Germany as one of the founders of that nation's independent living movement. Now married and the proud father of two young children, Uwe expressed great interest in the concept of a culture of disability, but questioned if Germans were ready for it. Yet, during the weekend we stayed there, we all attended both a rally advocating disability rights and Kassel's second, "*KRUEPPELPOWER* (Cripple Power) Festival." The first festival, a couple of years earlier, had been disappointing, on a rainy weekend that precipitated a low turnout. This time was completely different. Many people attended, even though a city-sponsored festival occurred in a different location at the same time.

We could stay only for part of the first of two days before traveling again, but in that short time we saw an English disability musician, Mat Fraser, described in

173

various ways as punk, hip hop or rap. He calls himself a "sad and bitter man with very small arms," in the header to lyrics from his tape, "Survival of the Shittest." Lyrics from a song about the movie industry called, "Blacking Up," include the following:

> This is a roll call of some actors in the movies
> Like Daniel Day Lewis who felt he had to prove his
> Acting craftsmanship in My Left Foot
> Couldn't that have been done by someone more suitable
> Not bodied but experienced in the soul
> The role we're told not really believable see
> From an actor that really had cerebral palsy—
> D'you remember when the white excuse for Othello
> Was "Black actors don't have that Shakespearian word flow"
> In reality knowing Desdemona kissed white lips
> Allowed the fantasy to be upheld by all the liberal racists
> Well their attitude's the same to all us cripples and freaks
> They want make-up and prostheses and thespian techniques.
> An able bodied actor takes the rostrum to applause—
> You justify apartheid by giving an award?
> And for all the "Oh come on now this man's hysterical with hatred'
> What else d'you call it when you're ostracized, denied and segregated?

The remaining acts we saw were German, including rockers Station 17. This group of developmentally disabled individuals formerly resided in an institution. Musicians were brought into the institution to give residents music therapy. These individuals were so talented they were assisted in organizing a band, and now are recording artists who have released Compact Discs and who travel all over Europe.

We also saw Jomi, a pantomimist who is deaf and who had the audience in stitches with his satire. We missed the most famous of the German musicians, Klaus Kreuzeder, a jazz performer who uses a wheelchair, playing with Sax as Sax Can. With many more musicians, performers, and exhibit booths this event was so successful plans were already being discussed for a third festival in 1999.

The next day we traveled west to Mainz, near Frankfurt, where I immediately joined a panel at the city's decades-old Open Air Festival. The Festival's theme was inclusion of everyone and we were delighted to hear the sounds of Station 17 once more. Tired from travel and work, we did not stay for most of this Festival, but the presence of disability was felt in the panel, in performers, and perhaps most importantly in the integration of many people with and without visible disabilities in every corner of the festival.

During the next week, we worked at the CIL in Mainz where we met Hans-Peter Terno who is a member of *Blindwuetig-Oder*, a cabaret revue. *Blindwuetig-Oder* uses a play on words and may be translated as, "blinded angry." As I discussed my interest in disability culture with Hans-Peter and others, I learned about a 1997 Festival called *Grenzenlos Kultur* (a culture without boundaries), which featured *Blindwuetig-Oder* and many other artists and activists with disabilities, including CanDoCo, an English dance company.

In our last weekend in Munich, I connected with the director and a member of the Munich Cripple Cabaret, who have produced plays, videotapes, and comic books, all addressing disability in a humorous vein. They include *Neues Aus Rollywood* a book whose title uses the German nickname for a wheelchair user, *Rolli*, to say New from Wheelchairwood, (instead of Hollywood), and the play *Krueckliche Tage* that uses the term for crutches to make the title, *Crutchi Days*, instead of happy days.

All of these artists and activities indicate there is a wealth of talent and culture in Germany, disability and otherwise. With a long history of intellectual attainments, as well as a belief in the importance of the arts that too few of us in the U.S. share, German disability culture has an opportunity not only to provide us with examples of the worldwide growth of this movement, but to address and atone, just as we Americans do, for an atrocious historical record of oppression and death to those who are different.

PART VI
Endings and Beginnings

A HEALING JOURNEY

[I conclude this collection, as I began, with an essay about my own health, my perspectives about Gaucher Disease, and how it is all intertwined throughout my life. After years of writing and talking about pain, I felt compelled to describe this journey once more a few years ago. Many changes had occurred in my life, including interactions with a variety of alternative healers. Interspersed in this essay is part of a long prose poem I wrote describing how it felt to try and move in the midst of a Gaucher bone crisis. I retain the poem in this essay because it is the best representation of the emotion of the moment, while the remainder of the essay is more distanced observation. It was published in the May/June 2000 issue of the now defunct *Disability Life*. While this is the final essay in this book, I continue to write. This piece is not so much an ending as another glimpse of life in process.]

I remember. I was a teenager. All pain. My pain was all pain. All pain was my pain.

I remember. Lying in the field kitty-corner to our house. Watching the dragonflies. Imagining interplanetary travel. Daydreams. Not too many night screams. Not yet.

Why did I start to limp? No one knew. I began to favor my right leg just before my sixth birthday. Hometown physicians in Kalamazoo, Michigan, could not locate a cause for the mysterious pain. My parents turned elsewhere.

Excited at the prospect of my first plane ride, I climbed up the stairs with my mother and grandmother. We traveled to Rochester, Minnesota's famed Mayo Clinic.

Doctors, who seemed to know my grandmother, biopsied both thighs and then informed my mother that I had Gaucher Disease (GD). The year of the diagnosis was 1957. Little was known about GD. In the post-biopsy conference, my mother heard the bits of knowledge physicians then possessed. An inherited, progressive, non-fatal condition, my parents and I could anticipate severe, chronic pain for the remainder of my life.

I lie remembering. My gangling body. Draped over chairs, couches. Upside down. Potato chips and Dr. Pepper. Bags of potato chips. Six packs of Dr. Pepper. Downed easily. One setting. No need to get up. Just continue reading, watching TV. Upside down. Watching the world with my head on the floor. My most comfortable position.

Returning home I behaved no differently than before. I played a game of football in the Michigan autumn. After being tackled I tried to get up. I could not. My leg was broken. Still unhealed from the recent biopsy, the femur—the long bone—in my right thigh snapped. A second adventure: spending my late October birthday and Halloween lying in the hospital waiting for the bone to heal.

I lie remembering. Torturous nights. Excruciating days. Once I slept for thirty-six hours. I woke every once in a while. But I lie in a hide-a-bed in the middle of the living room. Surrounded by people, TV, noise. Better to sleep; to escape. The pain of the house. The pain of the room. The pain of the body.

Each spring and fall, as the Michigan atmosphere changed, so would something inside my body. My right knee would swell to the size of two mammoth fists resting side by side. The pain was agonizing, excruciating. I have spent much of my life trying to describe it.

Numbing. I remember the numbing, mind-succumbing, all-encompassing pain. Twisted bones. Joints out of place. Bone infarctions.

That's what they call it now.

When I was a kid we called them "attacks." It fit. It felt right. My body attacked me and left me wounded, needing time to recover.

My left knee and then my hips joined in this chorus while I was still a teenager. The pain, as devastating as it is, never was the worst part of this condition. The inability of anyone to predict the course of the disease was its most frustrating aspect. I asked over and over again, of anyone who might know, what I could expect in the future. No one knew. Still advice flowed freely: "Find a job where you don't stress your hips." So much for my dreams of baseball stardom. "When you hurt, slow down, relax, give your body time to rest and recuperate." Both my external and internal guidance ignored this counsel. I was much too ambitious to slow down. I had a life to live. An income I would have to earn. How was I to become a man if I kept slowing down?

No weight bearing was possible.
Movement of any kind caused

excruciating, undulating waves
of pain. No movement was just
as bad. Constant, pounding,
searing, pervasive pain.
But I could not lie in my bed, alone,
all day and all night. I did not know
any esoteric, medical, or philosophical
reasons why. I just knew I could not lie
in my bed, alone, all day and all night.

I had to move.
Ah, there, was the rub.
Moving.
Slowly.
Excruciatingly.
Painstakingly.
Painfully.

I left home for college at the opposite end of the state of Illinois, where my parents had moved the summer before my senior year in high school. Two years later I fulfilled my own dream and moved west. I found myself in Tucson, finishing school, becoming engaged and married, and then moving to New Mexico for more school. In the mid-1970s we moved to Norman, Oklahoma, where we began a family. My wife, daughter, and I lived in a small house while I finished my doctoral studies in history.

I lived what passed for a "normal" life. Pain remained and intensified. It seemed like every one of my lower joints sang with pain. I constantly sought methods of relief. The codeine doctors prescribed when I was six had never been very effective. The Demerol of my young adulthood was better. But not great.

Once I counted. Literally. The minutes to move. Lying to sitting. Sitting to standing. Standing to moving. Over half-an-hour.

I am not making this up.

I am not attributing to memory something that did not happen.

I am writing this because so few do. But I am not the only one. There are others. My pain is not my pain alone. My pain is not all pain.

I lie. I decide to get up. To go to the
bathroom. To go to bed. To get something to eat.
To see another room. To do something. I decide to
get up.
Not I get up. No, this is not an unconscious movement.
This is very conscious, deliberate. It must be. It will
happen no other way.
I decide to get up.
I decide to get up.
I decide to get up.
Okay, I have decided to get up.
I move. I scream. I hurt. Maybe I won't get up. I am
paralyzed with pain.
Okay, I have decided to get up.
Okay, I have decided to get up.
Okay, I have decided to get up.
I move.
I scream. I hurt. I will get up. I will get up. I will get up.

A young man, in my late twenties, I had lived with GD for twenty years. But I had never gotten used to it. I continued to seek relief. Orthopedists recommended that I eventually have hip replacements, but to wait as long as possible for my bones and technology to be more compatible. When I finally grew so fatigued with the everyday pain, I asked my current orthopod how would I know when at last to have this surgery? His response was as depressing as informative, suggesting that when I felt so much pain at night that I could not sleep, even with painkillers, then it would be time.

I could still sleep with painkillers. But what about the misery of surviving each day?

I wondered aloud to my doctor about using a wheelchair. He advised me not to consider such a drastic alternative, stating that if I ever got into one I would never get out of it.

He saw me as my medical condition and gave what he believed to be his best medical advice. I had a much different perception of who I was.

I was a father who, because I couldn't stand the pain of walking and standing, did not enjoy accompanying my young daughter to her pre-school activities, or to the park, or to the mall. I was an active member of my community, who served on many Boards of Directors and participated in a variety of local activities. I had to function with as little pain or exhaustion as possible.

Too many days and nights of pain and fatigue convinced me to ignore my doctor and listen to my heart. I borrowed a wheelchair. Tentatively pushing myself towards freedom. Using a wheelchair quickly became a liberating experience. Malls no longer seemed like prisons designed to cause me as much agony as possible from one end to the other. The zoo beckoned. School functions were a breeze. Leaving home no longer meant continuous excruciating pain or debilitating fatigue.

> I move.
> I move.
> I move.
> My body begins to move with me. All of it.
> Except the knee.
> Slowly, deliberately, tenderly, consciously, painstakingly,
> carefully, cautiously, I lift my knee. I move it alongside me.
> I place it with the rest of my body.
> I drag it to a sitting position.
> I exhale.
> I rest.
> I sweat.
> I am exhausted.
> I hurt.
> I curse.
> I breathe.
> I hurt.
> I curse.
> I breathe.
> I hurt.
> I curse.

My spleen became enormous as the GD cells accumulated in that organ. My doctor suggested it be removed. She was concerned about my low platelet and white blood cell counts. I was anemic. I should be sick all the time. I was not, but I should be. I never got sick. I just broke bones. Still, let's remove the spleen before it causes more damage. I agreed.

I lost fourteen pounds. That's how much my spleen weighed. A picture of my no longer internal organ found its way into one of the medical books describing GD.

I didn't feel better. In fact, I felt worse. I never had any pain above the waist before. When I played a peaceful game of Frisbee, sitting down, I felt a muscle pull in my back. It refused to heal. An X-ray revealed I had broken a vertebra. Healed now, I had to be more careful in the future. I could not. I fractured another vertebrae.

I decide to stand.

I decide to stand.

I decide to stand.

Okay, I have decided to stand.

I move. I scream. I hurt. Maybe I won't stand.

I am paralyzed with pain.

Okay, I have decided to stand.

Okay, I have decided to stand.

Okay, I have decided to stand.

I move.

I scream. I hurt. I will stand. I will stand. I will stand.

I move.

I move.

I move.

My body begins to move with me. All of it. Except the knee.

Slowly, deliberately, tenderly, consciously,

painstakingly, carefully, cautiously, I lift my knee.

I move it alongside me. I place it with the rest of my body.

I drag it to a standing position.

I exhale.

I rest.

I sweat.

I am exhausted.
I hurt.
I curse.
I breathe.
I hurt.
I curse.
I breathe.
I hurt.
I curse.

I lie two thousand miles away from my home in Oklahoma. Surgeons installed Harrington rods, two steel poles on either side of my spinal column and infused my weak and crumbling bones with cowbone.

I decide to move.
I decide to move.
I decide to move.
Okay, I have decided to move.
I move. I scream. I hurt. Maybe I won't move.
I am paralyzed with pain.
Okay, I have decided to move.
Okay, I have decided to move.
Okay, I have decided to move.
I move.
I scream. I hurt. I will move. I will move. I will move.
I move.
I move.
I move.
My body begins to move with me. All of it. Except the knee.
Slowly, deliberately, tenderly, consciously,
painstakingly, carefully, cautiously, I lift my knee.
I move it alongside me. I place it with the rest of
my body.
I drag it alongside me as I move.

I exhale.

I rest.

I sweat.

I am exhausted.

I hurt.

I curse.

I breathe.

I hurt.

I curse.

I breathe.

I hurt.

I curse.

The pain that caused my hospital stay also ended my marriage. Neither my wife nor I could endure the constant pressure on our family. Nine years after our wedding ceremony we separated. We became joint custody parents and I continued with my job and my meetings—and my pain. Six years later personal traumas and professional dead-ends combined to convince me to leave Oklahoma. After fourteen years, I moved, at the end of 1990, to California.

I arrive.

I am exhausted.

I hurt.

I curse.

I breathe.

I hurt.

I curse.

I breathe.

I hurt.

I curse.

I await the next time I need to move.

I can wait for a long time, I think.

But, of course, I cannot.

A revolution in knowledge about GD has occurred since I was first diagnosed. In the 1970s, researchers identified GD as a metabolic disorder caused by an enzyme that was unable to eliminate lipid, or fatty, cells. The lipids accumulate in the body causing organs like the spleen and liver to enlarge, and bones to become weak. Known as Gaucher cells, in my body they have invaded primarily my bones and joints and precipitated states similar to osteoporosis and arthritis.

Recent research has isolated over forty different strains of GD, but all remain combined into three primary classifications. I have the most common form of the disease, known as Type I, or the Adult Form, because we anticipate average life spans.

When the Adult Form of GD affects someone from early childhood, pain is a common characteristic. I began writing about GD and pain when I was a teenager. In essays and poems, like the one integrated in this article, pain is dissected in its minutest forms. I began to write about pain for myself. To find an outlet. But I discovered when I tentatively approached the subject of pain in a speech, I struck a nerve.

Others had pain, but few would talk about it. People felt ostracized from admitting or discussing or conveying how pervasive pain had become in their lives. Audiences encouraged me to continue to talk about my experiences so that others too would have permission to share their feelings about pain.

About two years ago, after years of writing poems and essays and speeches about pain, I began to recognize a change in my relationship with pain. A process that I am only beginning to understand: I realize my thinking and my writing must have a new focus.

I still have pain. I am also healing.

◆   ◆   ◆

Researchers in the 1980s, having identified the low-producing GD enzyme, began attempts to produce a synthesized one. The new GD Foundation reported study results in its newsletter. I learned, soon after my move to California, that a new drug had indeed been synthesized to supplement the enzyme. My Oklahoma internist suggested I find out more about it. I did.

I had doubts.

I wondered whether side effects had been adequately investigated. I pondered the early data, which indicated people with internal organ involvement experienced better results than those, like myself, with damaged bones. Enzymes cannot be obtained orally. Availing myself of the synthesized drug was not as simple as swallowing a pill. Only intravenous infusions would work. Acquiring the enzyme meant spending several hours a couple of times a week in a doctor's office or hospital. GD had invaded my life enough. Did the possibility of relief have to feel as intrusive as the disease itself?

I had a busy job that required lots of travel. I wanted to spend no more time around doctors or hospitals than absolutely necessary. I concluded the treatment was not for me.

I stayed in California for three years. Great change ensued. I no longer felt able to function in a nine-to-five job. I explored the history of people with disabilities. I became passionate about disability culture, a belief that disabled people, like other minority groups, formed traditions and beliefs from their common experiences. I met an incredible woman and, much to my surprise and delight, remarried. My relationship with my daughter intensified, became strained, then virtually non-existent. Apart from my new marriage, I existed, but I did not thrive.

We decided to leave the hustle and bustle, and dampness of northern California for the slower pace of life and warm, dry climate of southern New Mexico. We sold our house, moved to a city where we knew no one, and created a not-for-profit organization, the Institute on Disability Culture.

Our lives did become more relaxed. The warm, dry air did feel wonderful. But I did not experience less pain. The opposite occurred and my pain escalated.

I slowly decided to investigate a new research protocol for the synthesized drug. A protocol that seemed tailor-made for me. The researchers sought someone my age who had no spleen and lots of bone involvement and had never used the synthesized enzyme. Still possessed with doubts about the entire synthesized enzyme process, I convinced myself that if I contributed to ongoing research as well as discovered any new information about myself and my condition it would be okay.

The research protocol required visits to both the National Institutes of Health and Massachusetts General Hospital, retracing my journey of a decade before. While I relived my back surgery and subsequent years, doctors performed volumes of tests. After a week of constant blood draws and X-rays and urine samples, I learned that I did not meet the protocol criteria. My bone density, one of the standards of evaluation, could not be measured, even on their high-powered equipment. Stunned by this news I wondered how I managed to get out of bed, to walk around the house, to get in and out of a car, or my wheelchair, with my fragile, paper-thin bones. The doctors just urged me to get Ceredase, the synthesized enzyme, as soon as possible.

I decided to check out the possibilities. We met with a representative from Genzyme, the drug's manufacturer, and after grilling him for a day I decided to give Ceredase a try. Shortly before my forty-fifth birthday I began to receive infusions.

The ordeal of the first infusion might have confirmed all my earlier fears. In my doctor's office, on a day she expected to see no other patients, she was suddenly unavailable. I waited for hours. When we finally did connect, she seemed more nervous than I, handling what was then the most expensive drug on the market. Five times she stuck me before she finally got the IV into my veins. I had never been stuck more than once before. I felt the liquid rushing into me and I made more trips to the bathroom in that two or three hours than I would have thought possible.

Finally, it ended. But what would this choice bring?

My wife noticed an almost immediate surge in my energy level. I noticed I could no longer take naps, even when I wanted to. My body temperature changed. I no longer became cold as easily. I used to dread stepping out of the shower, no matter how warm the day, because I would be so cold. No longer. Now I sweated as I eased out of the shower, without regard for how frigid the outside air might be.

A weight gain is usually the first sign that the enzyme is working, but for six months my weight remained the same as it had for the past twenty years. Then a transformation began. I gained about ten pounds. Blood tests, too, showed signs of improvements.

While I enjoyed my newfound energy and other signs of increasing health, my pain did not merely continue, it accelerated. After forty years of GD cells insinuating themselves in my bones, the enzyme which replaced them caused a change in my bone structure stimulating pain. In an ironic twist of fate, as I showed outward signs of improving health, the pain persisted and invaded my life even more than before.

Depression ensued. I feared that healing and pain would be paired together forever. Then my life changed again.

In August 1997, we traveled to Germany to visit friends for three weeks. Otto and Eva are both unconventional physical therapists who practice Integrated Manual Therapy, a technique combining a variety of healing practices. The friendship we have developed with them has dramatically affected our health.

Mid-way through the second week of our visit Otto and Eva introduced us to Knut and Ulrike. Believing their life mission is to find ways to decrease pain, they have sought techniques to fulfill this goal. Knut, an internist, explained to us they thought they had found an incredible, non-invasive therapy that reduced pain, called Pulsed Signal Therapy (PST).

An American physician and chemist, Richard Markoll, has concentrated on developing PST since 1980. Clinical studies at the Yale University School of Medicine affiliated teaching hospitals involved more than 5,000 patients. The idea behind PST is that when someone is born their cellular structure is designed in a certain way. As we live and grow, life traumas create pain in the cells around ligaments and tendons and change their cellular structure. PST machines contain an air-coil system that resembles a ring. Electro-magnetic signals stimulate one's body to rearrange cells to their original non-pain situations. PST is believed to decrease pain and increase functional capacity in conditions ranging from osteoarthritis and sports-type injuries to any joint or musculoskeletal disorder. No side effects have been discovered.

In the U.S., PST awaits FDA approval. In Europe, Knut became the first physician to install PST. He described treating many patients with varying degrees of trauma and achieving a success rate of about eighty percent in pain reduction. As a physician who never again expected to see people with our rare conditions, and as a healer who wants to alleviate pain, Knut offered us treatments. We accepted.

He explained that people need at least nine one-hour treatments. Two sessions in one day are possible, but only if spaced at least five hours apart. After the treatments end the process is believed to continue to work on the cells of your body for the next two to three months. The PST, if functioning well, will continue to have a positive impact for an extended period.

The day we began treatment we met an elderly woman who informed us that before she began the PST she needed a painkilling shot an hour before she could get out of bed in the morning. After a few sessions of PST she felt like dancing. We were eager to begin.

The idea is to start with the area of most pain, so my wife, Lil, who was born with an undiagnosed medical condition of displaced hips and hyper-extended joints, began with her hips. I started with my lower back. Since we both wanted to treat areas of our bodies that required lying down, we were placed in the same room on mattresses that could be changed to various positions under the ring.

Both of us felt our pain lessen during the treatments. I experienced more success. Pain persists and is still sometimes tormenting, but less so than before the treatment. The area of my lower back that was the target of the PST machine recovers from aches and pains much more quickly than before.

The treatment stimulated another kind of healing as well, more difficult to describe. Ulrike walked into the treatment area one day to ask how we felt. I responded that I thought my life had changed, from many years of discussing the intricacies of pain to the nature of healing. Although I could not offer a concrete explanation of this feeling, I had a strong sense that future work would focus on health, rather than pain.

The processes of the PST treatment affected more than my physical health. Looking back, I believe I recognized a healing journey.

I remembered the appearance of my disease toward the end of my fifth year. My most vivid recollection from that time of my life is being a carefree terror on a tricycle. I rode with abandon throughout our neighborhood, often crashing my three-wheeler. Scrapes and bruises were proud testaments to my prowess. At the same time, I was extremely sensitive emotionally, devastated at the slightest insult.

My parents worried about my feelings. They repeatedly scolded me to culti-vate less sensitivity to criticism. I was warned that if I could not harden my feel-ings life would be fraught with hurt. How does a small child, especially a small boy in middle class America in the 1950s, discern external censure from an innate ability to be intuitive about people and events around him? I began to inhibit all my feelings.

My parents, in their desire to protect me from pain, unwittingly asked me to shut out a part of myself. Neither they, nor I, could understand the impact of this advice. When I shut down this integral aspect of my personality I created space for another part of myself to become manifest. Suppressed, but ever present, my genetic disease, first appeared. Its advent compelled both myself and others around me to pay attention. No one could argue with the concrete evidence of swelled joints or broken bones. These pains were legitimate. They carried more weight than the invisible insights of a small boy.

Perhaps I had never before been ready to comprehend this exchange. Recalling this crossroads at the age of five is not laced with blame, but with a fiery desire to understand my life at this juncture.

The second bombshell occurred on a relaxed Sunday afternoon after we returned to New Mexico. We were not home alone though. Two different visi-tors from Germany had just arrived. Earlier in the day, one of these new German friends offered me a treatment of another non-invasive process called Metamor-phic Technique, consisting of light touch on the feet, hands, and head. A few hours after this procedure the thought that popped into my head, seemingly unbidden, I'm ready to make a home again. I wondered what that meant. Within seconds I knew.

A year earlier my daughter turned eighteen. We renewed contact. We had recently seen one another for the first time in five years. It was a wonderful reunion and we were becoming close once more. When I thought, I'm ready to make a home again, I realized I gave myself permission to put aside past guilt and regret concerning my own role in our strained relationship.

Today, I realize I am prepared to be whole again—perhaps for this first time since the age of five. A dictionary definition of health is being whole—or being in complete integration with oneself, physically, spiritually and emotionally. A lack of health then would be signified by a failure of integration.

For years in the disability rights movement I have worked toward societal integration, without much thought to my own intrapersonal integrity. I believe that I must now focus on internal synthesis.

I strive to stay true to my own personal journey of healing and becoming, while advocating for still needed social changes. In the past, I've found success concentrating on either myself, or the world at large, but not the two together. I now hope I'm able to find the path toward integrating my own personal life with that of the universe, of which we are all a part.

This is the healing journey on which I embark. If I am successful I will become whole, regardless of disability, or pain, or external demands.

I will be healed.

APPENDIX
DISABILITY CULTURE VIDEOS

Able to Laugh. 1993. 27 minutes. Produced by Michael J. Dougan. Available from Fanlight Productions, 47 Halifax St., Boston, MA 02130.

Six professional comics who have disabilities shown onstage.

Black Diamond. 9 1/2 minutes. Available from Melanie Media, 2951 Derby St. #101, Berkeley, CA 9470.

Afi-Tiombe Kambon performs the story of a child born with a disability to a woman in slavery.

Dancing from the Inside Out. 1993. Approximately 40 minutes. Available from Fanlight Productions, 47 Halifax St., Boston, MA 02130.

The video of this dance troupe, which formed in 1987, combines interviews of three dancers with disabilities with footage from a performance using the group's combined talent of people with and without disabilities.

Exploding Myths: Exploring the Emerging Culture of Disability. 1993. Available from Corporation on Disability and Telecommunications of Northern California, PO Box 1107, Berkeley, CA 94704.

A look at Bay Area artists, including Cheryl Marie Wade, Neil Marcus, and Bruce Curtis.

Here—A Poetry Performance. 1992. 13 1/2 minutes. Available from CM Wade, 1613 5th St., Berkeley, CA 94710-1714.

Cheryl Marie Wade performs her poetry.

Max and the Magic Pill. Circa 1995. 60 minutes. Available from Paraquad, 311 N. Lindbergh Blvd., St. Louis, MO 63141.

A look at Max Starkloff, founder of Paraquad, the Center for Independent Living in St. Louis, focusing on both his disability and his zest for a typical American life out of a nursing home and in his community.

No Apologies. 1995. 28 minutes. Available from Wry Crips, PO Box 21474, Oakland, CA 94620.

Moving, humorous performances from a 1990 show, interspersed with interviews with group members. Open captioned.

Mr. Roberts. Circa 1988. SIXTY MINUTES. Approximately 15 minutes. Available from World Institute on Disability, 510 16th St., Oakland, CA 94612.

Harry Reasoner interviewing Ed Roberts and his mother, Zona, discussing Ed's early years, his experience with polio and his decision to live, and the founding of the Physically Disabled Students Program, the Center for Independent Living, and the World Institute on Disability.

Positive Images: Portraits of Women with Disabilities. 1988. 58 minutes. Available from Harilyn Rousso, Executive Director, Disabilities Unlimited, 3 East 10th St., Suite 4B, New York, NY 10003.

Follows the lives and careers of three women.

"Redefining Ourselves." 83 minutes. Available from Corporation on Disabilities and Telecommunications/Northern California, PO Box 1107, Berkeley, CA 94704.

Includes *Here; The Moving Body,* featuring Bruce Curtis in experimental movement and dance; *The Commercial,* a comical look at how to avoid someone with a disability performed by Wry Crips Disabled Women's Theater; *Black Diamond; Migraine 2000,* featuring art work of Peni Hall; *Melvin's Brat,* a satirical look at TV tele-a-thons for kids with disabilities featuring Pamela Walker; and *Into the Echo Chamber/Dreamweave,* featuring six disabled artists collaborating on exploring the creative process and combining their music, dance, and poetry.

Tell Them I'm a Mermaid. 1982. 23 minutes. Available from Films Incorporated Video, 5547 N. Ravenswood Ave., Chicago, IL 60640-1199.

Victoria Ann-Lewis and six other women describe life as women with disabilities.

We Won't Go Away... 1981.

A look at the Section 504 demonstrations in San Francisco and the early independent living movement.

When Billy Broke His Head...And Other Tales of Wonder. 1995. 57 minutes. Produced by Billy Golfus and David E. Simpson. Open captioning available. Available from Fanlight Productions, 47 Halifax St., Boston, MA 02130.

WOW!!! Dare I say it? This *is* inspirational: includes activism, art, bureaucracy, family, friends, and a look at everyday life—all in a very funny hour.

ENDNOTES

"OH, DON'T YOU ENVY US OUR PRIVILEGED LIVES?" A REVIEW OF THE DISABILITY CULTURE MOVEMENT

1. Lyrics throughout the article are from Canadian Jane Field's song, "The Fishing is Free," which is also the title of her self-produced 1994 cassette.

2. See, "Deviants, Invalids, and Anthropologists: Cross-Cultural Perspectives on Conditions of Disability in One Academic Discipline: A Review of *Disability and Culture," Disability and Rehabilitation: An International, Multidisciplinary Journal*, 18 (5) (May 1996), 273-75; *Investigating a Culture of Disability: Final Report* (Las Cruces, NM: Institute on Disability Culture, 1994); "We Are Who We Are...So Who Are We? *MAINSTREAM: Magazine of the Able-Disabled*, 20 (10), (Aug. 1996), 28-30, 32, and "Poster Kids No More:" Perspectives about the No-Longer Emerging (In Fact, Vibrant) Disability Culture." *Disability Studies Quarterly* 18 (1) (Winter 1998), 5-19.

3. Pfeiffer, David, "Is There a Culture of Disability?" *1984 And Beyond, Proceedings of 1984 AHSSPPE Conference*, 1984 and Schein, Andrea "Is There A Culture of Disability?" *1984 And Beyond, Proceedings of 1984 AHSSPPE Conference*, 1984.

4. Examples include *Abilities: Canada's Lifestyle Magazine for People with Disabilities*, Canadian Abilities Foundation, 489 College St., Suite 501, Toronto, Ontario M6G 1A5, Web Site: http://www.abilities.ca/abilities. html?showabilities=1/; *Accent on Living* no longer publishes; *Disability International*, Disabled People's International, 748 Broadway Winnipeg, Manitoba, Canada R3G 0X3, Web Site: http://www.dpi.org/en/start.htm; *MAINSTREAM: Magazine of the Able-Disabled* no longer publishes; *Mouth*, Free Hand Press, Inc., 4201 SW 30th Street, Topeka, Kansas 66614-3023, Web Site: http://www.mouthmag.com/; *New Mobility: Life on Wheels*, Web

Site: http://www.newmobility.com, and *The Disability Rag's Ragged Edge Magazine*, PO Box 145, Louisville, KY 40201, Web Site: http://www.raggededgemagazine.com/.

5. Hooper, Ed, "Seeking the Disabled Community," *Disability Rag*, (Aug 1985), 1, 4-6, 8. Quote is on page 8.

6. In Mary Johnson, "EMOTION AND PRIDE," *Disability Rag*, Jan/Feb 1987, 1, 4-10. Quote is on page 9.

7. Published in Cheryl Marie Wade, ed., *Range of Motion: An Anthology of Disability Poetry, Prose and Art* (Albany, CA: Minuteman, a KIDS Project/ Squeaky Wheels Press, 1993). 25.

8. Hevey, David, *The Creatures Time Forgot: Photography and Disability Imagery* (London: Routledge, 1992).

9. Las Cruces, NM: Institute on Disability Culture, 1994.

10. See "A Celebration of Diversity: An Introductory, Annotated Bibliography about Disability Culture," *Disability Studies Quarterly*, 15 (4) (Fall 1995), 36-55, for what I considered the most important entries at that time. The current bibliographic count is 2443.

11. This is not to say that I am in total ignorance of international discussions relating to or specifically about disability culture. Two examples, which do not show up in the text of this article, but cover a number of different countries, are Barbara Duncan and Susan Brown, eds., *Personal Assistance Services in Europe and North America* (New York and Oakland: Rehabilitation International and World Institute on Disability, 1993) and Diane E. Woods, ed., *Traditional and Changing Views of Disability in Developing Societies: Causes, Consequences, Cautions* (Durham, NH: International Exchange of Experts and Information in Rehabilitation, 1993).

12. See also his cartoon books, *Digesting The Child Within* (New York: William Morrow, 1991), *Do Not Disturb Any Further* (New York: William Morrow, 1990), *Do What He Says! He's Crazy* (New York: William Morrow, 1992), *Freaks of Nature* (New York: William Morrow, 1995), *The Night They Say, was Made for Love, Plus my Sexual Scrapbook* (New York: William Morrow, 1993), *What Kind of God Would Allow a Thing Like This to Happen?!!* (New

York: William Morrow, 1994), and his fairy tale, *The King of Things and the Cranberry Clown* (New York: William Morrow and Company, 1994). Another cartoonist, whose books, and humor, is far less caustic, is Frank Warner's *Dis"ability" Joke Books* (available from Dis"ability" Magazine, 5910 Willis Road Palmetto, FL 34221 77th St. East, Palmetto, FL 34221, Web Site: http://disabilityjokebooks.50megs.com/index.html.

13. "Out of Isolation," (Berkeley: INTER-RELATIONS, 1985). The poem was also made into a video with the same title in 1989. Like most of Moore's visual art, it contains lots of nudity.

14. For much more from and about Frank and his work see his World Wide Web site: http://www.eroplay.com.

15. This is quite an oversimplification of both the demonstrations and how Section 504 has affected people. Although Scotch is the most comprehensive analysis of this transformation, not everyone who played a role in these activities agreed with his assessments and analyses. See John Hessler, "Letter to Editor," *Disability Rag*, Sept. 1985, 3.

16. Shapiro also has his critics, particularly of his emphasis on the Berkeley area. But his account is very readable and has begun to fill the broad gap of no mainstream publications about the disability rights movement.

17. Longmore, Paul K. and David A. Goldberger, The League of the Physically Handicapped and the Great Depression: A Case Study in the New Disability History. *The Journal of American History* 87.3 (2000): 73 pars. 23 <http://www.historycooperative.org/journals/jah/87.3/longmore.html>.

18. I've included in the text the ones I've read so far, but see also *Carnal Acts* (Boston: Beacon, 1996); *Voice Lessons* (Boston: Beacon, 1994); and *Waist High in the World* (Boston: Beacon, 1996).

19. See, "Deviants, Invalids and Anthropologists: Cross Cultural Perspectives on Conditions of Disability in One Academic Discipline: A Review of *Disability and Culture,*" in *Disability and Rehabilitation: An International, Multidisciplinary Journal*, 18 (5) (May 1996), 273-75, for my detailed review.

20. *Ibid.,* and in *Investigating a Culture of Disability*, 95-96.

21. In Edison J. Trickett, Roderick J. Watts, and Dina Berman, eds., *Human Diversity: Perspectives on People in Context* (San Francisco: Jossey-Bass, 1995), 244-60.

22. This is a subject which deserves much more detailed discussion and is only just beginning. For more detail on it and my disagreements with Scheer, see "We Are Who We Are...So Who Are We? *MAINSTREAM: Magazine of the Able-Disabled*, 20 (10), (Aug. 1996), 28-30, 32.

ZONA AND ED ROBERTS: TWENTIETH CENTURY PIONEERS

1. A fuller description of this experience is found in the introduction to this volume, *Gaucher Disease: A Personal History* and in my *Investigating a Culture of Disability: Final Report* (Las Cruces, NM: 1994), 69-70.

2. Joseph P. Shapiro, *No Pity: People With Disabilities Forging a New Civil Rights Movement* (New York: 1993), 56.

3. Zona Roberts interview by Steven E. Brown, Dec. 27-30, 1996, audiotapes (in Steven E. Brown's possession).

4. Roberts interview, side 2, tape 2.

5. *Mr. Roberts.* (Circa 1988). *Sixty Minutes.* (Available from World Institute on Disability, 510 16th St., Oakland, CA 94612).

6. Roberts interview, side 2, tape 4.

7. Shapiro, *No Pity*, 45.

8. Brown, *Investigating A Culture Of Disability*, 50-51, Steven E. Brown, *Independent Living: Theory and Practice* (Las Cruces, NM: 1994), 28-30, Shapiro, *No Pity*, 47-55.

9. Hale Zukas. "CIL History," presented at Independent Living Conference, October 21-23, 1975, Berkeley, CA. (in Steven E. Brown's possession).

10. Roberts interview, side 2, tape 6.

11. Ed Roberts interview by Steven E. Brown, Sept. 8, 1993, audiotape, side 2, tape 1 (in Steven E. Brown's possession).

12. Zona speculates that the murderer himself is probably long dead. Roberts interview, side 1, tape 7. In another conversation about the murder, Randy was described as stepping between the girl and the gunman, who was aiming at his date. Lillian Gonzales Brown, personal communication, Aug. 15, 1997.

13. This story was related at a small memorial service for Ed I attended at WID on March 20, 1995.

978-0-595-28893-
0-595-28893-6

29260780R00137

Made in the USA
Middletown, DE
12 February 2016